D1030896

GREAT
LEADERS
HAVE NO
RULES

CONTRARIAN

LEADERSHIP

PRINCIPLES

TO TRANSFORM

YOUR TEAM AND

BUSINESS

GREAT LEADERS
HAVE NO
RULES

KEVIN KRUSE

RODALE.
New York

Some content has previously appeared on the author's blog,
kevinkruse.com, and forbes.com.

Library of Congress Cataloging-in-Publication Data
Names: Kruse, Kevin, 1967– author.
Title: Great leaders have no rules : contrarian leadership principles
    to transform your team and business / Kevin Kruse.
Description: First Edition. | New York : Rodale Books, 2019. |
    Includes bibliographical references and index.
Identifiers: LCCN 2018038787| ISBN 9781635652161 (hardback) |
    ISBN 9781635652178 (eISBN)
Subjects: LCSH: Leadership. | Management. | BISAC: BUSINESS
    & ECONOMICS / Leadership. | BUSINESS & ECONOMICS /
    Management.
Classification: LCC HD57.7 .K7848 2019 | DDC 658.4/092—dc23
    LC record available at https://lccn.loc.gov/2018038787

ISBN: 978-1-63565-216-1
Ebook ISBN: 978-1-63565-217-8

Printed in the United States of America

Book design by Jen Valero
Jacket design by Sarah Horgan

10 9 8 7 6 5 4 3 2 1

First Edition

Amanda, Natalie, and Owen,

who already lead with empathy, kindness, and love

CONTENTS

FOREWORD

One of the most popular Dilbert comic strips in the cartoon's history begins with Dilbert's boss relaying senior leadership's explanation for the company's low profits. In response to his boss, Dilbert asks incredulously, "So they're saying that profits went <u>up</u> because of great management and <u>down</u> because of a weak economy?" To which Dilbert's boss replies, "These meetings will go faster if you stop putting things in context."

Great leadership is indeed a difficult thing to pin down and understand. You know a great leader when you're working for one, but even they can have a hard time explaining the specifics of what they do that makes their leadership so effective. Great leadership is dynamic; it melds a variety of unique skills into an integrated whole.

Great leadership often requires counterintuitive action in critical moments. This is where Kevin Kruse comes in. You see, Kevin has a remarkable ability to spot where leaders lead themselves astray and turn this knowledge into simple actions any leader can take to change the course of a career for the better. That's the beauty of this remarkable (and sorely needed) book.

It's pretty incredible how often you hear leaders complaining about their best employees leaving, and they really do have something to complain about—few things are as costly and disruptive as good people walking out the door.

Leaders tend to blame their turnover problems on everything under the sun, while ignoring the crux of the matter: people don't leave jobs; they leave bosses. Most leaders have good intentions, but, oftentimes, what you think you're supposed to do as a leader is a real morale killer.

Organizations know how important it is to have motivated, engaged employees, but most fail to hold leaders accountable for making it happen. When they don't, the bottom line suffers. Research from the University of California found that motivated employees were 31 percent more productive, had 37 percent higher sales, and were three times more creative than demotivated employees. They were also 87 percent less likely to quit, according to a Corporate Leadership Council study of over 50,000 people.

Gallup research shows that a mind-boggling 70 percent of an employee's motivation is influenced by his or her boss and 70 percent of employees consider themselves to be not engaged at work. It's pretty easy to see the opportunity.

Leadership is the art of persuasion—the act of motivating people to do more than they ever thought possible in pursuit of a greater good.

It has nothing to do with your title. It has nothing to do with authority, seniority, or one's position in the hierarchy of a company. Too many talk about a company's leadership while referring to the senior-most executives in the organization. They are just that, senior executives. Leadership doesn't automatically happen when you reach a certain pay grade. Hopefully you find it there, but there are no guarantees. You can be a leader in your workplace, your neighborhood, or your family, all without having a title.

Leadership has nothing to do with personal attributes. Say the word *leader* and most people think of a domineering, take-charge, charismatic individual. People often think of icons from history like General Patton or President Lincoln. But leadership isn't an adjective. We don't need to be extroverted or charismatic to practice leadership. And those with charisma don't automatically lead.

Leadership isn't management. You have fifteen people who report to you and P&L responsibility? Good for you; hopefully you are a good manager. Good management is needed. Managers need to plan, measure, monitor, coordinate, solve, hire, fire, and so many other things. Managers spend most of their time managing things. Leaders lead people.

You're not a leader just because you have people reporting to you. And you don't suddenly become a leader once you reach a certain pay grade. A true leader influences others to be their best. Leadership is about social influence, not positional power.

So don't wait for the title. Leadership isn't something that anyone can give you—you have to earn it and claim it for yourself.

This book will help you do just that.

Travis Bradberry, PhD, author of
Emotional Intelligence 2.0

INTRODUCTION

I know two things about leadership that most people do not believe.

First, leadership is a superpower.

Second, almost everything we've been taught about leadership is wrong.

Lack of leadership at work drove my first two companies into the ground. And leading effectively enabled me to go on to start, build, and sell several multimillion-dollar companies.

Lack of leadership at home ended my marriage. Family leadership enabled me to raise three amazing kids as a single dad.

Lack of self-leadership had me walking around half asleep, overweight, and depressed. Leading myself first now has me healthy, focused, and energized.

If you are following traditional old-school management advice, you will derail your career or derail your family or both.

Today our budgets are smaller and head count is fewer but we are asked to do more. We must navigate an environment impacted by merciless change, ceaseless 24/7 communication, and younger generations who have dramatically different values than their parents.

This book has one purpose: to teach you how to be both the boss everyone wants to work for and the high achiever every CEO wants to hire—all without drama, stress, or endless hours in the office.

The advice you're about to read is grounded in solid research and based on my entrepreneurial experience starting and growing companies for the last three decades. These are companies that have won Inc. 500 awards for fast growth, as well as "best place to work" awards for employee satisfaction.

It's also based on my interviews with over two hundred guests on the *LEADx Leadership* podcast. I've gleaned real-world wisdom from management gurus like Dan Pink, Liz Wiseman, and Kim Scott; CEOs like Jason Fried of Basecamp, Mike McDerment of FreshBooks, and Jim Whitehurst of Red Hat; military professionals like submarine commander David Marquet, combat pilot Vernice Armour, and US Army major Joe Byerly; and productivity experts like Rory Vaden, Jeff Sanders, and Craig Ballantyne.

I started the LEADx Academy (www.leadx.org) with the vision of providing world-class leadership education to anyone, anywhere, *free of charge*. I believe leadership is the greatest force for good. Through online training, articles, and podcasts LEADx has already helped people in 192 countries to realize that leadership is not a choice. If leadership is influence, it means all of us are leading those around us every single day.

To get the most out of this book, I encourage you to do three things.

First, suspend disbelief. Every chapter is filled with advice and tactics that go against conventional wisdom. You will hear your inner voice exclaim, *I could never do that—that would never work in my company!* Pay that voice no mind. You can overcome that cognitive dissonance by questioning the effectiveness of your current leadership approach, and by testing out your new superpowers one at a time.

Second, download the *Great Leaders Have No Rules* Action Plan (www.LEADx.org/actionplan). It will provide a great overview to the content and will help you to apply new concepts at work and at home.

Third, read this book (of course). Without disbelief, with the action plan, chapter by chapter you will soon become the boss you always wished you had yourself.

Kevin Kruse
Philadelphia, PA, 2019

GREAT
LEADERS
HAVE NO
RULES

1

CLOSE YOUR OPEN DOOR POLICY

On May 10, 2017, TV talk-show host Steve Harvey broke the internet.

Not literally of course. From social media to the nightly news, people expressed outrage over what *Variety* called a "shocking memo" sent by Harvey to his staff (Wagmeister 2017). With blunt language, he let everyone know to leave him alone. He wrote in part:

I'd like you all to review and adhere to the following notes and rules for Season 5 of my talk show.

There will be no meetings in my dressing room. No stopping by or popping in. NO ONE.

Do not come to my dressing room unless invited.

Do not open my dressing room door. IF YOU OPEN MY
DOOR, EXPECT TO BE REMOVED.
My security team will stop everyone from standing at my
door who have the intent to see or speak to me.
I want all the ambushing to stop now. That includes TV
staff.
You must schedule an appointment.

While his memo went viral and there was universal shock, I
was shocked that everyone else was shocked.

Steve Harvey was right.

Could he have phrased it differently? Absolutely. Even my
teenagers know all caps is never a good idea.

Realize that Harvey is sixty years old and hosts a radio show,
a TV talk show, *Family Feud*, *Little Big Shots* talent show, and
various other programs. He routinely travels between Los An-
geles, Chicago, and Atlanta to produce these programs. He is a
father and a grandfather.

I'm ten years younger and need a nap just from thinking
about his schedule.

Everyone on Steve Harvey's staff should know better. They
need him to be energized, funny, and creative. They don't
need him to micromanage show details or to be signing au-
tographs.

It's shocking he had to send the memo at all. Doesn't he
have a highly paid assistant—serving as chief of staff—to op-
timize his time? Why isn't the show producer acting as the
gateway to the rest of the staff?

You can tell that the memo was written with emotional honesty, in a time of frustration. But he wasn't wrong.

"GOT A MINUTE?"

While I may not be a talk-show host I can definitely relate to the problem of unscheduled "pop-ins."

The three-word question that used to send chills down my spine: "Got a minute?"

I'm working on next year's strategic plan and budget. How will my company go from $5 million in annual sales to $10 million in a single year? That's the goal set by my strategic partner— who will fund the growth—and it's up to me to show how we're going to do it.

Let's see . . . if I add two more sales reps in column X, at $90,000 a piece, and they each increase sales starting in month six by—

Knock, knock, knock. "Got a minute?"

I want to be supportive of my team members. I want to be a good leader. So . . .

"Sure, Tracy, what's up?"

She steps in and displays a 3-D picture of a conference ex-position booth. "I'm getting ready to approve the final booth design. They made the changes we asked for last week. Does it look okay to you?"

"I told you last week it looked good to me with the changes."

"I know, but this is the final *final* design. Before I go spend $10,000 I thought I should check—"

"Tracy, you got this. Budget is fine, design is fine."

"Okay. Thanks."

I sigh.

Okay, where was I? Impact of hiring more sales reps. What column was the number of sales reps on this sheet? There— column X. If I add two reps—

Knock knock. "Got a minute?"
Really?!

IN SEARCH OF COMMUNICATION AND TRANSPARENCY

An open door policy refers to the practice of business or organizational leaders leaving their doors open so that employees feel welcome to stop by and meet informally, ask questions, or discuss matters that have been weighing on their minds.

These days, with open office environments, coworking spaces, and remote team members working around the globe, the "open door policy" is more metaphorical than ever before. The equivalent of walking through a physical open door in many organizations is now: sending an SMS phone text message, a direct message on Facebook or Slack, an instant message on Skype, or a ping on Basecamp.

Regardless of whether the interruption is through an actual door or a digital door, the theory is that an organization uses such openness to build a culture of trust, collaboration, communication, and respect regardless of an individual's position in the hierarchy. Access to executives should reduce workplace gossip and rumors.

The goals of an open door policy are admirable; who wouldn't want that?

But while the goals are noble the disadvantages are real. When I surveyed a hundred thousand subscribers to my newsletter and online community, I was flooded with stories of open doors gone awry from managers and individual contributors alike.

BUT I DON'T WANT TO SPEAK UP!

Do team members really want an open door?

Over a decade ago, University of Virginia professor James Detert and Harvard professor Amy Edmondson set out to discover why some employees bring ideas to their managers and others don't. They interviewed approximately two hundred people in a high technology company and discovered that about half of them chose to hold back from sharing information that could be beneficial for the company (Detert and Edmondson 2007). Why? The professors explain:

> In a phrase, self-preservation. While it's obvious why employees fear bringing up certain issues, such as whistle-blowing, we found the innate protective instinct so powerful that it also inhibited speech that clearly would have been intended to help the organization. In our interviews, the perceived risks of speaking up felt very personal and immediate to employees, whereas the possible future benefit to the organization from sharing their ideas was uncertain. So people often instinctively played it safe by keeping quiet. Their frequent conclusion seemed to be, "When in doubt, keep your mouth shut."

Detert and Edmondson found that some workers referenced company myths of individuals who publicly shared their ideas and were "suddenly gone from the company."

Indeed, Gerry is one of my readers who emailed me to describe what happened when he used the open door policy of his manager's manager.

In a meeting with him, I told him about some of the problems of performance and communication we had with my immediate manager who was new and inexperienced. I also suggested some solutions . . . a few days later he told my manager what I said. That created a bad situation between the two of us. My manager soon left the company and a few months later I also was forced to leave.

Is there any substance to these stories of being fired for using the open door? In reality, it doesn't matter. If the perception is there, then the danger of employees holding back is guaranteed.

Whether conscious or unconscious, employees are weighing the potential risk against the potential reward. Only if the benefit far outweighs the risk will they then proactively walk through the open door. Putting the responsibility on those individuals to openly communicate their problems or suggestions is keeping half your team members silent.

LEAPFROGGING THE CHAIN OF COMMAND

If only half the people in the corporate world feel comfortable with the open door policy, it may be even worse in the military, especially when the open door policy is used to leapfrog one's direct leader and take an issue to a higher level.

The concept of the open door policy is even written in the US Army's command policy. Army Regulation 600-20, chapter two paragraph two, instructs, "Commanders will establish an open door policy within their commands . . . The timing, conduct, and specific procedures of the open door policy are determined by the commander" (US Army 2014).

But even though it's an official written policy—a requirement of command—soldiers are still making the same risk-to-reward analysis described by professors Detert and Edmondson. And most of them seem to think it's not worth the risk. A random sampling of views from military message boards include:

- "You can't trust higher-ups. They often say they have open door policies. Their open door policy should be used with extreme caution. Whatever you say will be used against you. I have met a lot of higher-ups with 'open door policies,' but from their records, the 'open door' policy felt more like a 'trap door' policy." (K 2012)
- "The most common problem is that troops feel there will be backlash after using the open door policy. Maybe not directly, but indirectly" (Shephard 2014).

Even in the business world, it's easy to understand how leapfrogging the chain of command comes at great risk.

Let's say you have a problem with your boss, Fred. Or maybe you just have a great idea that you feel Fred isn't taking action on. So you go "above his head" to discuss the issue with his boss, Judy. In most organizations, one of two scenarios are likely to play out and neither of them is good for you.

> JUDY: *"Did you take this issue to Fred? You did? Okay, well, I agree with his decision, now get back to work."* And now I know you are a whiny troublemaking employee with bad judgment.

Or,

> JUDY: *"Did you take this issue to Fred, your boss? You did? Well, I'm glad you persisted and brought it to my attention. I'm going to override his decision and let him know that we need to take _____ more seriously in the future."*

And then your boss, Fred, will be thinking about you: *I always knew they were a whiny troublemaking employee.*

Can your boss fire you? Probably not. Can he ignore you, give plum assignments to others on your team, give your work extra scrutiny, deny your request to work from home on a snow day, and otherwise make you miserable? Yep.

You lose in either scenario.

WHY ATHLETES DON'T TALK

It isn't often that a Rutgers sports team gets highlighted by ESPN or receives national attention. As a 1989 Rutgers College graduate I should know. So I wasn't entirely surprised in 2013 when the national coverage of Rutgers turned out to be for a very bad reason.

ESPN's *Outside the Lines* program aired highlights from hours of video showing Rutgers basketball coach Mike Rice verbally and physically abusing players during practice sessions (Van Natta 2013). Rice can be seen pushing several players, almost choking one and kicking another, and throwing basketballs at their heads from just a few feet away. Verbally, he belittled them with obscenities and homophobic slurs. Initially Rutgers fined Rice and suspended him for three games; once the video went viral, Rice was fired. The player abuse at Rutgers lasted from 2010 to 2012 before it was discovered.

More disturbing are the cases of young athletes being sexually abused by coaches or staff members. Jerry Sandusky at Penn State. Larry Nassar, former USA Gymnastics team doctor, who was convicted of sexually abusing over a hundred girls for more than twenty years.

Often, when these horrific incidents eventually come to

light, I hear adults—parents—say something like, "Why didn't the kids tell someone?"

Once again: risk versus reward.

Players fear being benched, cut from the team, hazed, or even worse. College athletes are afraid of losing scholarships. In cases of sexual abuse there are the associated emotions of embarrassment and shame. All this is weighed against the very real possibility that accusations won't be believed, or the abuser won't be stopped. Indeed, in the case of Nassar it turns out many of the young gymnasts had told parents, coaches, and trainers of their abuse but in many cases they were just told that they were lucky to be in the care of such an esteemed doctor, he was giving them legitimate medical care, and they shouldn't pursue it further.

An "open door" policy is passive. What's needed is an active, safe communication policy. How many athletic directors send anonymous surveys to all their players specifically asking about hazing, bullying, or abuse? Could a player upset about not getting more game time use the anonymous survey to make false accusations? Of course. And a single data point could be viewed as what it is. But if an athletic director, a league president, whoever, sees a large percentage of players making the same accusation, then it can be investigated and acted upon as necessary.

I'D BETTER CHECK WITH THE BOSS FIRST

For some employees the problem isn't fear of going through the open door, it's that they *always* want to go through that door. In their willingness to share all their problems and ideas and decisions with management, these individuals become overly dependent on company leaders. In essence, they become afraid to make most decisions without first running them by their superiors.

Legendary leadership coach Marshall Goldsmith explores the reasons for this in an essay he wrote for the *Harvard Business Review* (Goldsmith 2010). As Goldsmith points out, employees know their jobs better than anyone else in an organization. But not everyone is comfortable making decisions, and here is the critical point:

> It isn't possible for a leader to "empower" someone to be accountable and make good decisions. People have to empower themselves. Your role is to encourage and support the decision-making environment, and to give employees the tools and knowledge they need to make and act upon their own decisions. By doing this, you help your employees reach an empowered state.

Oftentimes, an open door policy is a lazy (and inefficient) substitute for the initial investment of training and attention that your employees need. When you give your people the tools and coaching they need to make good decisions, that's what they'll do.

In contrast, if you neglect those people in favor of a policy where they can just come get you when they need you, you hinder their development and ability to make decisions.

Nick, a manager in a family business in Australia, tried to modernize the company culture partly through a wide-open door policy. He described the outcome:

> I was working seventy-plus hours a week, I had unwittingly created a culture of dependence whenever even the smallest

problem arose . . . The stronger (more valuable) staff members did not feel empowered or even trusted in their roles and were more likely to consider leaving. And the weaker (less valuable) staff members only grew more dependent. Which meant the stronger staff would leave and the weaker ones would stay. It would appear that my open door management policy had basically become a mechanism by which staff could delegate their problems back onto management!

As a leader, you have a responsibility to pass on valuable knowledge and experience through good training and coaching—*at appropriate times*. But leaving the door open discourages your people from appropriate bias-to-action and limits the opportunities they need to grow.

DRAMA AND THERAPY

This productivity problem is magnified when limits aren't placed on what the open door should be used for.

I interviewed leadership expert and bestselling author Cy Wakeman for *The LEADx Leadership Show* about the cost of lost productivity that comes from workplace drama. She amusingly told me that people drive through the open door policy in their BMWs—Bitching, Moaning, and Whining. She said, "I realized pretty quickly that the open door was a portal for drama. It catered to ego, fueled feelings of victimhood, and contributed to low morale" (Wakeman 2017).

Paul is a plant manager who shared with me his challenges with team members who bring in personal issues. He said:

[It's] a complete double-edged sword. On the one hand, I know for the most part what makes my employees tick, and I try to be as open and honest with them as I can about things. On the other hand, I've had to sit and listen to men cry about what their girlfriend or wife did to them, how disrespected they feel, why they have to have the next day off, and the list goes on. Because I probably went a little too far with my open door policy the line between an understanding boss and a "might-be-a-friend" has been blurred.

I once had a submarine commander tell me that any person under his command could sink his sub, so it was his job to know exactly what was going on with everyone on board—at both a professional and personal level. But if your team doesn't carry the same risks, having an open door that allows people to enter for any reason can quickly spiral out of control.

A PRODUCTIVITY NIGHTMARE FOR MANAGERS

Employees aren't the only ones harmed by traditional open door policies. In fact, it's team leaders and executives who reap the most adverse effects. As you might imagine, the open door policy makes for a productivity nightmare. Various research studies indicate the typical office worker is interrupted fifty to sixty times per day, and the average time between interruptions is about three minutes.

A manager named Connie told me her team complains if she isn't always around and available. Her frustration comes through in her email:

I am a manager with an open door policy. The biggest downside I am facing is that I can't get things done. Every task I want to work on takes forever to be completed—this of course affects my productivity, my emails, and my sense of achievement.

Another manager, Tina, told me, "Although I support the open door policy, it means that every time I am interrupted it takes me fifteen minutes to get back to what I was doing."

Researchers who study productivity have varying estimates of the impact of interruptions. On the high side, Gloria Mark, a professor of informatics at the University of California, found that it takes an office worker an average of twenty-five minutes to fully return to a task after being interrupted (Mark et al. 2008). And that research doesn't address how interruptions affect the quality of our work.

It doesn't take a mathematician to see how even a few unplanned meetings can destroy your flow over the course of a day.

SHOULD THE OPEN DOOR BE SLAMMED SHUT?

So with all the problems that come with an open door policy, is it time to slam these doors completely shut? Should leaders refuse unscheduled one-on-one meetings? Should they remain distant and aloof?

Of course not.

The danger is in poorly trained managers accepting the open door policy in its most simplistic definition. Many methods can be used to enhance the policy or to supplement it to fulfill the goals of transparency, collaboration, and trust. The open door policy can be fixed.

OPEN DOOR SOLUTION #1: SCHEDULED OFFICE HOURS

As we've seen, traditional open door policies can quickly lead to major productivity losses for managers and executives. But what if a simple tweak could maintain all the benefits of the open door policy, without being a productivity killer?

If your door is always open, even figuratively, you never know what your day is going to look like. In contrast, keeping the door open only during limited and preset times allows you to keep control and prevents others from interrupting your flow. Additionally, by reducing the opportunities of being available, you force your people to trust their instincts on smaller matters and to seek guidance or advice only if the issue is large enough.

You may consider setting one day a week as your "open door" day. Choosing Monday has the advantage of making sure everyone has the information or decisions they need to have a productive week. If you're already using your Mondays for one-on-one meetings (a very good practice), then Friday would be a good day to choose enabling everyone to end the week by clearing their mind.

Others I know choose one hour each day to be their "open door" time. If you try this, consider your own productivity needs first. When are you most productive? For most of us, that would be in the morning. You may consider your "maker" hours to be before lunch and your "manager" hours after lunch.

OPEN DOOR SOLUTION #2: SET THE GROUND RULES

Pope Francis might have an open door policy, but if you want to speak with him in his office, you'll walk past a sign that reads, VIETATO LAMENTARSI. In English, COMPLAINING FORBID-DEN (Tornielli 2017).

The Italian newspaper *La Stampa* ran a picture of this sign on the pope's apartment door, given to him by an Italian self-help author, Salvo Noe. In small print the sign also reads, "Violators are subject to a syndrome of always feeling like a victim and the consequent reduction of your sense of humor and capacity to solve problems."

Although displayed in jest, it's a valid reminder to bring the pope possible solutions along with your problems.

Karen Baetzel, CEO of BattleAxe Consulting, spent thirty years in the US Navy as an aviator. She told me that she set specific ground rules for the men and women in her command:

> I think the unqualified open door is an invitation to organizational turmoil. What I think is much better policy is a "half-open door," and when I was commanding officer, I would explain exactly what that meant. It meant you could come to me:
> 1. When the traditional chain of command is not working the way you know it is supposed to work, not when you didn't get the answer you wanted
> 2. When you think something unsafe, illegal, or un-American is going on
> 3. You understand the consequences of misusing or trivializing the privilege

Nick, a manager in Australia, discovered that his wide-open door policy was leading to dependency, he implemented the "two-solution" rule. He explained, "At the very least, all of our staff has now been made aware that they are never to come to management with a problem, unless they can propose two or three possible solutions. If they can't, I ask them to go away and come back to me when they can."

And what about those leapfrog meetings? You know, someone from several levels "down" the organizational chart has leapfrogged over her boss and into your office. One anonymous commander in the US Navy described his approach on the RallyPoint message board (LCDR 2016):

> If what they bring up is something that is a CoC (chain of command) issue, I always ask them, "Have you asked your chain of command?" If the answer is no, I send them off to utilize what the military has in place for a reason. If the answer is yes, I ask them if they've utilized their entire chain. I have yet to see an issue that couldn't be resolved by utilizing the command structure.

And for those individuals who have a gift for noticing everything that could be better—and bringing it to your attention—simply agree with them and put them in charge of the solution. In recent years I've exclaimed:

- "You're right, Carl, our proposal pricing worksheet is far from perfect. Why don't you take a crack at adding the functionality you are looking for and let me look at it a month from today."
- "You're right, James, we might be missing an opportunity to enter the K-12 market. Why don't you do some research and take first crack at a business plan and we'll review it together."
- "You're right, Mike, our writers should understand the sales process better. Why don't you convene a series of 'lunch and learns' so we can close that gap."

Not surprisingly, many of these "issues" seem to disappear when the person who noticed the problem has to come up with the solution.

OPEN DOOR SOLUTION #3:
THE WEEKLY ONE-ON-ONE

When it comes to forging quality communication that benefits both you and your direct reports, few tools are more powerful than the weekly, prescheduled one-on-one.

Scheduled one-on-ones take away the "unexpected" element of an open door policy and provide something that would otherwise be missing: the chance to prepare. By preparing for each of these meetings, you can tailor your assistance to the needs of the individual, maximizing personal impact.

Just remember the one-on-one is actually the employee's meeting. You're here for them. Great questions include: What's on your mind? What are your most important tasks for the week? How can I help? What do you need to be successful?

Furthermore, these weekly meetings enable you to build rapport and stay in touch on big personal items on an ongoing basis. As a type A introvert, none of my team members would ever consider me warm and fuzzy. But my first question every Monday is usually a simple, "How was your weekend?"

OPEN DOOR SOLUTION #4:
A CADENCE OF COMMUNICATION

Although the one-on-one is of primary importance, it's just one piece of the puzzle if you're looking to build a culture of effective communication. Additional meetings should include:

- Weekly team meetings
- Monthly division meetings
- Quarterly all-company town halls

The goal should be to build a scheduled rhythm of communication that encompasses all employees, no matter how "high" your position in the hierarchy. These group meetings provide information or context to all team members.

While asking "Are there any questions?" is acceptable, remember that people may be wary of speaking up in a public setting. One technique to overcome this is to hand out index cards prior to the meeting and invite people to write anonymous questions on the cards, which are then passed forward to be answered.

Individuals will be less likely to walk in unscheduled to ask you about the latest rumor or the status of a specific initiative if you are already addressing these types of issues on a regular basis.

THE TAKEAWAY

Communication and problem solving are admirable goals but the traditional open door policy is a passive effort, utilized by only half of all workers. It can also discourage autonomy, empowerment, and reduce the productivity of managers.

A more effective solution is to schedule more limited "office hours" and weekly one-on-ones, to proactively solicit the opinions of quieter team members, and to actively foster an environment of trust.

The bottom line: the more frequently you communicate and ask questions of your team members, the more they'll come to believe that you care and it's a safe environment to bring things to your attention.

In case you still have reservations about shutting your open door, perhaps you should consider this feedback from Melinda, a very astute manager, who sums it up best:

> I prefer my boss and even my colleagues to keep their doors closed when they are so busy they don't have time to talk. I would rather have their wholehearted attention when I have something to discuss with them than feel that their door is "open all the time." Open doors do not equal open minds.

HOW MIGHT YOU APPLY THIS IF YOU'RE A:

MANAGER: Consider scheduling fifteen-minute one-on-one meetings with each member of your team, once a week. Make them recurring appointments on the same day each week so you, and your team members, can rely on the cadence of communication. If you have more than a dozen direct reports, meet with each team member every other week. Let them know that with this added meeting rhythm, you are reducing your "open door" hours to just an hour a day. Remember to frame the change in the spirit of enhanced communication and empowerment.

SALES PROFESSIONAL: It takes a lot less time and effort to sell more to existing customers than it does to find new customers. Whether you are an account director with multimillion-dollar corporate accounts or a network marketer supporting downline associates, consider establishing a monthly or quarterly account review. For smaller transactional-type sales, this might consist of a simple email. For large corporate accounts, it might consist of a full-day on-site meeting. Remember, about half your customers will answer "fine" if you just ask them how it's going. You need to ask smart, probing questions. You want to find the pain points they're experiencing so you can assist before the problem gets bigger and they start buying from someone else.

SPORTS COACH: Given the culture of athletics and the traditional coach-athlete relationship, it is especially rare for players to proactively go to coaches with problems or ideas. During team meetings at practice or after games, consider calling on each player to contribute ideas on what the team did well and what areas should be worked on in the next practice. Consider meeting weekly with the team captain(s) who is likely to know the real issues on the minds of the players.

MILITARY OFFICER: Use a policy memorandum to make explicit your expectations on the open door policy. Let those under your command know that you expect them to first try to resolve any issues with their senior noncommissioned officer and that you require they notify their chain of their desire or intent to meet with you. Practice an "active open door" by walking among those you command.

PARENT: Ideally from a young age, create the habit—the tradition—of eating dinner together each night at the table. Impossible? How about a big, long family dinner each Sunday. Game night once a month. Minivacations each quarter: a day of fishing, a baseball game, a father-son shopping spree. Become adept at asking questions that elicit actual responses. Teens can be especially challenging. If you ask, "How was your day?" You'll surely get the "fine" response. Try instead, "Tell me about the best part of your day." Or, "What happened in the book you're reading for school today?" And I'm surprised how often I strike gold with, "So what's the friend drama and gossip this week?"

INDIVIDUAL: Who are family members and friends whom you love the most? Do you communicate haphazardly whenever you remember? Consider establishing a consistent rhythm of communication: midday text messages and weekly date nights with your spouse, monthly "first Sunday" brunch with your siblings or parents, quarterly BBQs or parties with your friends from college. Ask the probing questions you really want to know about. Don't assume they don't want to talk about it; they might be assuming you don't want to hear it!

B e honest. Do you check your smartphone for text messages or emails during business meetings?

If you do, according to researchers at the University of Southern California Marshall School of Business, you are probably annoying your boss and peers (Washington, Okoro, and Cardon 2013). Their study looked at the views of 554 full-time working professionals who earned more than $30K in income and were employed by companies with at least fifty employees. They asked participants about the use of smartphones in formal and informal meetings to uncover attitudes about answering calls, writing or reading emails or text messages, browsing the internet, and other mobile-phone-related behaviors. Key findings included:

- 86% think it's inappropriate to answer phone calls during formal meetings.
- 84% think it's inappropriate to write texts or emails during formal meetings.
- 75% think it's inappropriate to read texts or emails during formal meetings.
- 66% think it's inappropriate to write texts or emails during any meetings.
- At least 22% think it's inappropriate to use phones during any meetings.

Furthermore, the research indicates that older professionals and those with higher incomes are far more likely to think it is inappropriate to be checking text messages or emails during meetings of *any* kind. In larger organizations, this means that the "higher-ups"—you know, the ones who hold your career in their hands—are the ones who are likely to be most critical of your phone behavior.

While workplace etiquette and civility are important, when it comes to smartphones, these issues are dwarfed by the problems related to focus, attention, and productivity. We routinely take these little disruption devices and put them in our pocket, walk with them in our hand, and set them within eyesight on our desks. How did this come to be?

WHY FACEBOOK DOESN'T HAVE A PHONE NUMBER FOR CUSTOMER SUPPORT

Have you ever wondered why there is no technical support phone number for Facebook? You know, you're trying to figure out how to change your privacy settings but it's too complicated, or you want to upload several photos into an album but don't know how. Why can't you call up a customer service agent?

There is no phone support for Facebook because you are not the customer. You are the *product* they are selling!

If you just had an OMG reaction like when you found out Bruce Willis was dead in *The Sixth Sense*, you're not alone.

Facebook has customers, of course; they have four million of them. Four million advertisers from Coca-Cola and Walmart to your local pizzeria. Your little phone screen is the big TV screen of old. According to a report by eMarketer, annual spending on digital advertising worldwide is $224 billion, and most of that is advertising on mobile phones (eMarketer 2017).

To be fair there is no phone support for Google, Instagram, Snapchat, or Twitter, either. They all make money when they get your attention—that's the only way you'll see an advertisement on their platform. And they—and all the other "free" app makers—all employ a small army of supersmart people who are paid to get your attention as often as possible.

These are the people who run thousands of behavioral experiments to discover the things that increase your engagement with your phone: push notifications, little numbers in red circles indicating new messages, never-ending scrolling feeds, leader scoreboards, and even swipe left or swipe right. Some people call this work "user experience design" (UX) and some call it "gamification." Still others refer to it as "brain hacking" or even "mind jacking."

THE BIOLOGY OF ADDICTION

What do gambling, sex, drugs, and smartphones have in common?

Dopamine.

It's been called the love drug. Dopamine is a chemical released in the brain to reinforce pleasurable activities. And it turns out we get a dopamine response from the simple activity of checking our phone throughout the day.

Many make the comparison to pulling the lever on a slot machine. With every pull—every phone check—we're wondering, what are we going to get this time? And the fact that you don't win every single time is what makes it fun. It makes it addicting.

Psychologists refer to this as the effect of variable rewards. It's the anticipation. Maybe the last three times you looked you only got boring pictures of other people's food, political rants, and other people's kids doing supposedly cute things. But every now and then . . . jackpot! Goats doing yoga! Your joke got five more likes! Your sister left a comment, "LMAO"! A baby elephant chasing some birds! Dopamine dopamine dopamine, yay!

More than 40 percent of people check their phones within five minutes of waking up. Then we check our phone on average forty-seven more times throughout the day, and 30 percent of us check the phone right before going to bed. Young adults use their phones eighty-five times a day, over five hours of total time. All these findings are according to survey research conducted by Deloitte in 2015. It kind of makes you wonder what we did all the time before smartphones were invented!

SMARTPHONES DISTRACT AND DIMINISH BRAINPOWER

In March of 2012, Bonnie Miller was enjoying a stroll with her husband and son. She remembered she needed to reschedule an appointment so she used her phone to send a three-word text message and promptly walked right off a pier into Lake Michigan. Her family jumped in to help keep her afloat and within minutes the Coast Guard arrived to help her out of the water (Flacy 2012).

Our addiction to our phones can be seen daily. Cars swerving in the lane ahead as the driver checks her smartphone. The couple in the restaurant looking down at their phones instead of at each other. People staring down instead of up at concerts, parties, and sporting events. People walking into objects and each other on city sidewalks. It's kind of funny except when it isn't. Like when a woman who was texting fell off a cliff in Alaska and died in 2012 (Flacy 2012). The man who was distracted by his phone before falling to his death in San Diego on Christmas Day in 2015 (Quinn 2015). The woman who almost died falling off California's highest bridge while taking a selfie (Preuss 2017).

Half of all managers believe smartphones are the number one killer of productivity, and fully 75 percent of managers believe that their workers are losing two or more hours a day because of distractions according to a survey conducted by the Harris Poll (CareerBuilder 2016). In the same survey, the majority of employees reported that they didn't even have work email on their phones. So what are they doing on their phones during the day? Sixty-five percent admitted to personal messaging, 25 percent admitted to playing games, and 4 percent even admitted to watching porn (who admits to that?).

It turns out even if you don't pick up your phone to take a call, read a message, or (ahem) watch porn, just getting a notification of a call or text is enough to distract you. Cognitive researchers at Florida State found that people were three times more likely to make mistakes in their work if their phone notified them of calls or text messages—even if they didn't pick it up (Stothart 2015). This decline in performance was similar to those who actually took the call or read their new message. The researchers described their findings as "shocking" and explained that, "Although these notifications are generally short in duration, they can prompt task-irrelevant thoughts, or mind-wandering, which has been shown to damage task performance."

That's why I always silence my phone and even flip it over on my desk when I'm working.

But it turns out that's not good enough. Even having our phones near us is distracting—even if it's turned off!

Researchers at the University of Texas at Austin conducted a study with 548 undergraduates to find out if just having your phone nearby was consuming some of our cognitive resources (Ward et al. 2017). All the participants were instructed to "turn your phones completely on silent; this means turn off the ring and vibrate so it doesn't make any sounds." Then the participants were randomized into three groups: one group kept their phones facedown on their desks, another put their phones in their pockets or purses, and the final group had to leave their phones out in the lobby. Participants then completed a series of tests on a computer that are designed to measure cognitive capacity.

The group that had their phones out in the lobby performed significantly better than the group who had their phones in their pockets or purses. And the phones-in-the-pocket group significantly outperformed the group that had their phones on their desks. Professor Adrian Ward, lead researcher, explained that "as the smartphone becomes more noticeable, participants' available cognitive capacity decreases. Your conscious mind isn't thinking about your smartphone, but that process—the process of requiring yourself to not think about something—uses up some of your limited cognitive resources. It's a brain drain."

SMARTPHONES CONTRIBUTE TO STRESS

Biologically, dopamine is only half our addiction equation—our craving for pleasure. The other half comes from cortisol, known as the "stress hormone." It is released by the adrenal glands in response to fear or stress; it is considered a crucial part of our primal fight-or-flight mechanism.

When it comes to smartphones, many of us have FOMO, or "fear of missing out." Even if we aren't using social media for fun, we relentlessly check our email inbox, text messages, and Slack channels because we'll feel anxious if we don't. In 2017, the American Psychological Association released a study, *Stress in America*, showing that "constant checkers" were about 20 percent more stressed than those who don't check frequently. Those who check their work emails on the weekend were about 50 percent more stressed (American Psychological Association 2017). You may be tempted to check your inbox at night and on the weekend to relieve stress, but the "check-in" just reinforces the habit and anchors a never-ending cycle.

For a news segment called "Brain Hacking," journalist Anderson Cooper got wired up with electrodes to measure his physiological state, and while wired up, researchers were sending him text messages without him knowing it was part of the experiment. He could see his phone, and every time it pinged with a new text message, not only was he distracted, but his stress response spiked on the monitor (Cooper 2017).

And we don't need to be seeing our messages to feel the stress spike. Not seeing them can be just as bad. I can remember my fifteen-year-old daughter, Natalie, stressing out while on a family vacation. We were on a cruise ship heading for Bermuda, unlimited drinks, food, games, movies—a massive ship to explore! So what could be the problem? No Wi-Fi. There is even a term for this: nomophobia (from "no mobile-phone phobia"). Research conducted by the UK Post Office discovered that 53 percent of mobile phone users feel anxious when they can't find their phone, can't connect to a network, or when their battery runs out.

The specific problem for my daughter Natalie was that without Wi-Fi she couldn't use Snapchat, putting her "Snapstreaks" in jeopardy. The brain hackers at Snapchat cleverly created a feature that tells you how many consecutive days you've chatted with someone on the app. If your friend doesn't respond to a message within twenty-four hours, the chain is broken. Maintaining streaks is totally meaningless, and totally addictive.

I exaggerated when I said the cruise ship didn't have Wi-Fi. It did. But it cost an extra $25 per day per phone to access it. With myself and three kids I made the decision to only get Wi-Fi for myself. (You know, um, because I needed to check work emails once a day. Yeah, that's why.) Once Natalie discovered this, she immediately came up with a solution to her Snapstreak crisis. "Dad, I need to borrow your phone and log in to Snapchat . . ." In doing research for this book I learned that kids often solve this vacation problem by giving their log-in credentials to friends who can log in on their behalf and keep the streaks alive. Natalie hadn't thought of this idea prior to our trip, and I shared my phone with her once a day to keep the streaks alive.

Psychologically, maintaining streaks of activity is a relatively easy way for us to feel a sense of pride and accomplishment. They take some time to build, are easy to compare and to brag about, and are easily broken (thus the stress and fear triggers).

The fear of breaking a streak can be used to keep us addicted to our apps but can also be used to help us maintain healthy habits like going to the gym on a string of consecutive days.

This story about Snapstreaks on the cruise ship happened two years ago. Yesterday my thirteen-year-old son, Owen, came back from a week of sleepaway camp. "How was it?" I asked. "Do you think you'll keep in touch with some of the kids you met?"

Without hesitation he answered, "Oh yeah, I already have Snapstreaks going with a bunch of them."

SMARTPHONES CONTRIBUTE TO ACCIDENTS AND FATALITIES

You're on your back being wheeled into the operating room. It's cold, bright, the doctors and nurses scurry around in their scrubs. The anesthesiologist stands by your side and says, "Okay, you're going to go to sleep now." As you begin to drift off the doctor says one more thing. Don't worry about anything. I'll be right here . . . making three phone calls, sending thirteen text messages, and I'm going to check the internet thirty-six times.

Crazy? That's the phone activity of an anesthesiologist during a procedure to fix a sixty-one-year-old woman's defective heart valve. Normally a routine procedure, the patient died on the operating table (*Inside Edition* 2015). The malpractice lawsuit is ongoing.

The case seems shocking, but "distracted doctoring" is more common than you would think. The patient of a neurosurgeon who made ten personal phone calls while conducting brain surgery ended up paralyzed and the lawsuit was settled out of court. Over half of heart monitor technicians admit to making personal calls or sending text messages during surgeries and 40 percent of them even admit that it's unsafe (Chow 2011). Yes, smartphones enable health care professionals to access patient records, call for advice, look up prescribing information. But they can also distract and lead to medical errors.

For most of us, the distraction caused by our smartphone just means mistakes on paperwork and a loss of productivity. But in many industries, mobile phone distraction can lead to bodily harm or even death.

SMARTPHONE SURVEILLANCE IMPEDES CANDOR

As a young boy I had a hardcover book that covered the history of espionage, from World War II spies to U-2 pilot Gary Powers. I loved that book. My favorite chapter was all about the cloak-and-dagger technology. How cool would it be to have a secret microphone in a light bulb! How could I turn my shirt button into a camera?

Today, we are all potential spies. We walk around with highly sophisticated recording devices in plain sight. Touch the red circle, place the device in front of you on the conference room table—just like everyone else does—and leave the meeting with a recording of every word uttered in the room. Video isn't much harder.

Want to really make sure you don't get caught? Just go to the App Store and download an app that will record hundreds of hours of audio in the background—no lights, no sounds, no squiggly lines on the screen—so if anyone does look at your phone they would have no way of knowing. What does this "top secret" audio recorder cost? Ninety-nine cents.

And if you think it doesn't happen in your workplace, read the recent headlines that cover media moguls, members of

Congress, Radio City Music Hall dancers, locker rooms, Silicon Valley CEOs, and an endless number of teachers:

- "Ex-Fox Anchor Gretchen Carlson Secretly Recorded Meetings with Roger Ailes, Caught 'Numerous Incidents' of Harassment on Tape" (Gregorian 2016)
- "Secret Recording of Republicans' Closed-Door Meeting Reveals Fears About Repealing Obamacare" (Lange 2017)
- "Rockettes Management Blasts 'Deceitful and Cowardly' Dancer for Secretly Recording Team Meeting" (Flood 2017)
- "Listen Up, Coaches: Watch Out for Hidden Recording Devices" (Sondheimer 2017)
- "In Video, Uber CEO Argues with Driver Over Falling Fares" (Newcomer 2017)
- "Students Secretly Taping Angry Teachers" (Fox News 2007)

Now in the cases of these headlines—when most things hit the press—it's because a boss, coach, teacher, or other person of power is doing something illegal, unethical, or just plain dumb and embarrassing. That's not the point. I'm not worried about smartphones catching you doing something you shouldn't be doing. I'm not trying to protect union-busting executives or whistle-blowers who film the abuse of animals in R&D labs.

I am worried about open and honest communication in our daily work experience. I'm worried about self-censorship in matters where the fear is unfounded. Will people freely share crazy ideas in the spirit of brainstorming if they fear someone in the room might release audio clips in the future?

Matt Kincaid is an executive, a business professor at Heritage University, and the author of *Permission to Speak Freely: How the Best Leaders Cultivate a Culture of Candor*. He told me in an interview conducted for *The LEADx Leadership Show*:

> Research shows, as we take higher leadership roles, that actually people are less honest with us, less direct with us. We just don't get the candid things we need . . . people are hesitant to ask questions. They're hesitant to share their uncertainties. They're hesitant to offer up their own ideas.
>
> Things would be a lot easier and a lot better if there was no such idea as saying things the right way, because what that requires people to do is then run their authentic feelings and thoughts through a filter, we call it Verbal Photoshop (Kincaid 2017).

"Verbal Photoshop." Love that term.

Discrimination, abuse, bullying, and harassment should never be tolerated. Bad guys should be taken down with the help of secret recordings. But in this hypercompetitive dynamic world we live in, as leaders we need our teams communicating quickly and authentically, taking risks, and sometimes, yes, speaking with emotional honesty.

ARE SMARTPHONES REALLY A LEADERSHIP PROBLEM?

Do you care about productivity?

Do you care about the stress levels—the health—of your team members?

Do you care about the safety of your team members?

Do you care about a culture of candor, creativity, and fostering innovation?

If you care about any of these things, then smartphone use at work is a leadership issue.

IT'S TIME TO PUT YOUR SMARTPHONE AWAY

As a leader, your actions speak louder than your words. Your behavior influences the behavior of others. This chapter opened with survey data suggesting we shouldn't bring phones into meetings of any kind, because even just looking at messages is perceived by many to be rude. We now know that the constant interruptions of new emails and text messages and calls are hurting our productivity and the quality of our work. Even if our phones are muted nearby, we suffer "brain drain" because we have to focus on not responding to them.

Here's a radical idea: when you get to the office in the morning, mute your phone and put it in your desk drawer. (True, research would suggest that we need to leave it out in our car or give it to our assistant, but hey, I know that's entirely too radical!) Give yourself permission to check it three times a day, but after checking it and responding to any new messages, put it back in your desk.

But what if my spouse has an emergency and needs to reach me? It is amazing that somehow we survived for centuries without our family members being able to communicate in any given second. But regardless, maybe your spouse can call you on your regular office phone, or the landline phone of your assistant, the office receptionist, or your buddy at work?

But what if I use my phone to take notes and access the calendar during meetings? Discover the wonderful old-fashioned highly tactile world of quality pens and leather-bound notebooks.

You'll look sophisticated and research shows handwriting notes is better for both comprehension and recall (Mueller and Oppenheimer 2014). Later, type your notes into Evernote or whatever electronic system you use, or just snap a picture of your notepages at the end of the day and save them in your favorite note-keeping app. Keep a paper printout of your day calendar and monthly calendar in the back of your notebook to reference during the day.

But I'm in sales; don't I have to respond immediately if a client calls? I've had clients all my life and I, too, used to drop everything to pick up a client's call on the second ring. Eventually I realized they were hiring me for many different reasons, adding up to my total value proposition, and not so much because I pick up their phone calls the fastest. I now onboard new clients with a simple message: I love you and pride myself on great customer service, and I try to be superproductive on behalf of you and my other clients. To that end I check for emails and calls three times a day so I'll never be out of touch more than a few hours. It's always best to schedule meetings and calls in advance of course, but if they ever really need to reach me, they can call my assistant who will track me down.

SMARTPHONES, SAFETY, AND SULLY SULLENBERGER

For the one-hundredth episode of *The LEADx Leadership Show* I was honored to have as my guest Captain "Sully" Sullenberger. I ended the interview with the same last question I ask all my guests. "Help us to become a little bit better," I said. "Give us a challenge. What is something specific you want us to do?"

Would the man who successfully landed US Airways flight 1549 in the Hudson River—thus saving 155 lives—remind us to always keep our seat belts on when flying, or to really know where the closest exit is? Recently he's been fighting against the efforts of some in Congress to privatize the air traffic control system. He has called airline lobbyists "rats in dark corners." Maybe Sully will challenge us to call our members of Congress to protect airline safety.

Or will it be something about self-driving cars? Sully is the only independent member of the US Department of Transportation's Advisory Committee on Automation in Transportation. While he supports technology for driver assistance, he's against removing the driver from the controls completely.

But Captain Sully's challenge wasn't related to any of those things. In fact, he insisted on giving us two challenges, and both were related to our use of mobile phones. First, he advocated that we break our Pavlovian reaction to text messages and new emails in order to think more deeply and to build up our "creative reserves." He said:

> If we as leaders and team members set aside some period of time every day, perhaps half an hour or an hour, to free ourselves of distractions, to open our minds, to maybe even go outside for a run during lunch and not just react to whatever is immediately in front of us from email to a text, we have the ability to tap creative reserve . . . we can sometimes come up with the insights, the framing of a question in such a way that we come up with a solution we wouldn't have thought of otherwise (Sullenberger 2017).

His second challenge had to do with texting while driving:

> Right now, for the first time in decades, traffic deaths are on the increase. I'm convinced it's largely due to distractions

from personal electronic devices while we're driving. The single most effective thing that each of us could do right now, today, to stop that trend is to turn off, to mute, to put away our phones when we drive. And do what we did ten or fifteen years ago, wait until we get there to find out what's going on. Put our own needs aside, delay our gratification, delay responding to our need for curiosity for a few minutes, and that little gift of civic virtue would save thousands of lives in this country alone every year. We don't have the right to put others at unnecessary risk for our own convenience.

As leaders, for reasons of safety and reasons of problem solving, Captain Sully Sullenberger is asking for you to put that phone away.

THE TAKEAWAY

The combination of the internet and smartphones provides us with an unprecedented connection to information, entertainment, colleagues, family, and friends. The ubiquity of smartphones—and the never-ending stream of new message notifications—now leads to chronic distraction, which impairs productivity and can jeopardize safety. Leaders should model the way by silencing their phones and keeping them out of sight.

HOW MIGHT YOU APPLY THIS IF YOU'RE A:

MANAGER: Set the example for team members by not carrying your phone wherever you go. When you are meeting with someone, practice active listening and don't try to multitask with your phone. Display a NO SMARTPHONES sign in the conference rooms and encourage people to stay focused and productive throughout the day.

SALES PROFESSIONAL: Even if you legitimately need your phone for client calls more than most knowledge workers, try to "train" your clients to communicate in a way that will minimize your disruptions and maximize your productivity. If you call them to check in midweek, they'll be less likely to call you. If you schedule your phone calls with them ahead of time, they'll begin to mirror the practice back when they want to call you.

SPORTS COACH: As a coach you have considerable authority over your players. Just let them know that whether they are on the bench during a game or in the locker room afterward, you expect everyone to be phone-free and focused on learning.

MILITARY OFFICER: Smartphones have many benefits in the military just as they do in the private sector, but of course they come with added intelligence and operational security risks. Those are generally understood. The ongoing challenges are back on base: the dangers from texting and driving, work-life balance issues from never-ending messages. When deployed in combat, be mindful of and proactively handle casualty notification knowing that the ubiquity of smartphones gives you little control over information flow.

PARENT: I will admit that I occasionally glance at my phone when stopped at a red light, but I never check the phone when my kids are in the car. First, because I don't want to crash and hurt them and second because I know they're going to be driving soon and if I use my phone in the car, they'll think it's okay for them to do the same. No phones at the dinner table is another easy rule that will enhance communication and family bonding. Another powerful practice, hard to adopt, is to just not use your mobile devices at all when your children are around. Psychologist Catherine Steiner-Adair asked over one thousand children between the ages of four and eighteen about their parents' mobile phones. The dominant response was some form of anger, sadness, or loneliness, and other studies show a correlation between parental phone use and children acting out for attention. We'll have plenty of time to scroll through Facebook when our kids have moved out of the house; it will happen faster than we realize.

INDIVIDUAL: The single easiest, most life-changing thing you can do right now is to shut off all notifications on your phone. Instead of responding to every beep and vibration, like Pavlov's dogs to a bell, you will look at your phone when you want to. Now for most, that's still going to be way too often. I personally challenge you to a digital detox. Scared? You can always go slowly. Put your phone in another room tonight when you sit down for dinner. Leave your phone in your car for two hours as you watch your daughter's soccer game. Don't check work messages after 9:00 p.m. Never check it in the presence of your children. Soon you'll be ready to detox for an entire weekend.

'm staring at my expense check and it's short by about four dollars. Must have totaled it up wrong when I submitted my expense report.

I pull up the original form with a month's worth of mileage, meals, hotel rooms, and office supplies. I add up all the rows again and it seems correct.

This was the first time I had ever done my expenses and gotten a check back. I sold my business just a month before and was now a vice president and partner in the new company that acquired mine. Maybe I filled out the form wrong or don't understand how the expense stuff works. I shoot an email off to our chief financial officer letting him know that my check didn't match my submission; I didn't care about the four dollars but wanted to make sure I hadn't made an error somewhere.

The email I got back from the CFO—the person who was a fellow partner in the firm, the person who had just cut me a check for over a million dollars to buy my little company—said, "I deducted $4.34 because we don't allow employees to buy Post-it notes."

What? He actually reviewed my office supplies receipt and deducted the Post-it notes? And what the heck could be wrong with Post-it notes? I emailed back: Why?

And he answered: Wasteful expense. Cheaper to tear regular paper into little squares.

I can still remember how I felt although this was over fifteen years ago. Let's just say I sure didn't feel vice presidential or like a co-owner of the company. I mean, I didn't even have the authority to choose office supplies.

I wasn't the only one surprised by the expense reimbursement rules. Another executive, whose company had also recently been acquired, found his expense check short by five dollars because he had ordered a beer along with his dinner while he was traveling for business. He learned, after the fact, that the company policy was not to reimburse for alcohol. You could buy a five-dollar milkshake with your dinner but not a five-dollar beer.

What I had stumbled into would quickly become known as the "Post-it note debate." It wasn't about little self-sticking pieces of paper, of course. And it wasn't about beer. It was about rules.

While the partnership would eventually review and rewrite our internal policies (more on this below), very quickly the senior leadership divided into two camps. We of course thought they were "those out-of-touch micromanagers in HQ" and they thought of us as "those wasteful spendthrifts who don't care about the bottom line."

BAD RULES START WITH THE BEST OF INTENTIONS

All of us can rattle off countless "dumb rules" we've encountered in the workplace. But nobody creates rules that are dumb on purpose. Whoever created the rule must certainly believe they are doing so for the benefit of the organization. So where do all the rules come from?

Assuming the best of intentions, rules are implemented to maintain quality, high performance and standards, and also to mitigate risk.

You decide to start your own company. You are employee number one, and there are no others, so you need no rules. You, of course, know right from wrong and trust your own decisions.

It's a year later, your company is growing, and you now have ten employees who report to you. You still don't need rules, because whatever your personal whims, you are still able to personally hire, train, coach, and manage all the company employees. I can remember when I had ten team members and no official "rules," but everyone knew that I wanted the office phone answered by the third ring, casual dress was fine unless clients were in the office (then we wore suits), and we couldn't start our marathon games of *Doom II* until after 3:00 p.m.

Your company keeps growing and you now have 110 employees; ten still report to you, but each of your direct reports is now a manager of ten more people. And you also have more clients, more products, and more at risk. There are too many people and too many things demanding your attention. You can no longer personally hire, train, and coach every single employee yourself.

Suddenly, you notice things you don't like. Angela sent out a proposal with typos in it. Sloppy! Mei, while on a business trip, paid $700 to stay one night at the Ritz-Carlton. Wasteful! David wore cargo shorts and sandals and had his Hawaiian shirt unbuttoned to his waist when a client was in the office. Unprofessional!

So, to make sure this never happens again—in order to maintain quality—you help everyone by sending an email:

> **Team, in order to preserve quality, professionalism, and profits I am issuing a few rules.**
>
> All proposals must be proofread by Doris before being sent to a client.
>
> While on business travel, you must stay in a Motel 6 or cheaper.
>
> Dress code: No open-toed shoes, no shorts, no unbuttoned shirts.

Despite the best of intentions, despite how reasonable these rules seem, we know how this ends.

Soon, your company loses a sale because Doris was out sick for a week and couldn't check the proposal for typos. The Motel 6 in Duluth had no vacancy, so instead of spending an extra $10 to stay at the Super 8 motel next door, your employee spent $250 on a rental car to drive four hours to a Motel 6 that did have vacancies. Oh, and your managers are now walking around examining everyone's shoes and debating how many undone buttons at the top of a shirt or blouse is "unbuttoned."

Policies and rules are a natural phenomenon as a company grows; the business becomes more complex, the quality of new hires tends to go down, and communication with top leadership becomes more difficult. Even in small companies rules quickly multiply in the spirit of consistency—as a way to institutionalize the beliefs or standards of the CEO. And in large companies, policies and rules multiply like rabbits in an attempt to prevent or de-risk lawsuits.

Law firms that specialize in employment law spread the message that companies need more policies and contracts. From one law firm's website, "It is in every employer's best interest to protect itself from potential litigation by using every resource possible. An employee handbook is one tool that can aid employers in defending against such claims." The irony is that most handbooks expand to a length that even the HR team can't tell you what's in them anymore.

RULES REDUCE ACCOUNTABILITY

Leadership guru, and my personal mentor, Bill Erickson frequently says, "every rule takes away the opportunity to make a choice." As more and more of the job is dictated by processes, policies, and regulations, employees will feel less and less ownership over their work, and their emotional commitment wanes. The fewer choices people have—the fewer chances to make a decision—the more they'll think it's your company, and not their company.

Coach Mike Krzyzewski has been the head coach of the Duke Men's Basketball Team since 1980. "Coach K" has led the team to more NCAA tournament wins than any coach in history and has more championships than any other coach except the legendary UCLA coach John Wooden. And yet Coach K considers himself less of a basketball coach and more of a leader who happens to be involved with basketball. In his five books, radio show, and speeches to corporate audiences, he repeats the theme that leaders should strive to have the players care as much about the team as the coach does.

When it comes to rules, Coach K believes, "Too many rules

get in the way of leadership. They just put you in a box . . . People set rules to keep from making decisions" (Krzyzewski 2001). And, further, Krzyzewski maintains, as he told Greg Dale in an interview for the Championship Coaches Network, that there is a danger: "You become an administrator of rules rather than a leader. So, the first thing is to not have too many rules" (Dale n.d.).

Jessica P. told me she once had a boss who wouldn't even let her choose her own writing implement.

> I once worked for a woman in a health care setting and she thought that everything had to be written with a specific brand of pen in black ink. She didn't think that this was her rule—she believed that this was a well-known rule that everyone believed. She made me rewrite anything that didn't appear in the special pen ink—and refused to buy these pens for the office. The rule was pretty unmotivating and certainly had me questioning my job selection. In case the health care setting threw you off—and you thought I was doing something important like writing prescriptions or working on patient charts, nope, I was in marketing and the writing I was doing was for the internal team only.

Similarly, rules and processes can even take away the opportunity to voluntarily do the right thing. Lauren is a teacher at an international school in Asia who shared this story:

> In the school calendar there is an International Spring Fair. This is an amazing highlight of the year. Families and students come together to run tables and put forward the best food their country has to offer. There are booths every-

where, crafts, goldfish, jumping castles, you name it. As a part of the school community I was really looking forward to volunteering and enjoying the day with my husband and children.

So a shared document was created so all booths could be looked after. Here comes the dumb rule from administration, "You have to volunteer for at least two hours. I expect everyone to be there. I will be watching you, and checking. You don't have to but I will notice if you don't, it won't look good." In one swipe the possibility of really enjoying the day was ruined. Taking the power away to choose made the day tiresome and another day at work. We fulfilled our obligations and then went home. It is interesting that a dumb rule had as great an effect on morale as it did.

When something is forced, it takes away the pride and joy of participation from choice. Management, once again, snatches defeat from the jaws of victory.

RULES CAUSE SUFFERING TO MANY, TO PROTECT AGAINST THE FEW

Another problem with rules is that in an attempt to protect against a small minority, you decrease trust and increase hassles for the majority. Nick is a business owner in Australia. He shared a story that perfectly illustrates this point, and it turns out Nick is the one who created the "dumb" rule. He told me:

> I employ ten staff in three teams, all having access to laptops to perform their daily duties. I defined and distributed a technology policy that strictly prohibited the use of personal email, social media, etc. on those work laptops.

Then in my infinite wisdom, I installed various software controls on each laptop to ensure the policy was not circumvented.

This resulted in countless lost hours for me and my staff due to these overzealous controls that not only blocked social media applications, but just about everything else. Standard software updates were blocked, required websites were blocked, and other work-related applications, too. Each one of these incidents required my "Administrator Password" to allow staff to proceed. It was a productivity disaster.

In a similar story, Heidi wrote to me about the corporate rule that, while trying to protect against the minority offenders, prevents an entire department from doing their job. She explained:

> Our entire department's focus is on emerging customer-facing digital technologies. Yet we are not given access to any social networks, or sites like Slideshare, when connecting from our office network. To get access to the sites we use to do research, we have to raise a ticket with Group IT Services, and get director approval on the request. This practice is archaic and counterproductive, considering we actually need access to do our jobs.

RULES PUT FOCUS ON ACTIVITIES, NOT OUTCOMES

The third major problem with rules is that they are applied to activities when what really matters is outcomes. This is a common management mistake. For example, in an attempt to make sure employees are giving a full day's worth of work, there are often rules against working from home. But who's to say workers sitting in their cubicles aren't playing solitaire on their computer, checking Facebook on their phone, or hiding out in the bathroom?

Shelley is a real estate professional who works from home, along with her husband, on a real estate team. Their boss, in an attempt to teach customer service, inadvertently communicates distrust, which fosters disengagement.

> Our boss insists that we answer all emails from her well within an hour, answer texts within two minutes, and answer calls immediately. Always. From 7:00 a.m. to 10:00 p.m., seven days a week. Her reasoning: she wants us to be in that habit so that we respond to clients that quickly. I think this is bad because she is grossly controlling of us. We are not people who take customer service lightly. We are superresponsive. We are possibly workaholics!!! But to micromanage . . . that just makes us feel like she is waiting to yell at us. (Which she does.) I take Sundays off, and she agreed to that, but she insists that my husband answer my emails for me on Sundays.

Andrew Crookston shared his experience with rules as an IT professional, and some lessons from a mentor who fought against rules and policies. Crookston explained that many software companies will have a blanket rule for the percentage of code that needs to be quality checked with test scripts (instead of trusting the software engineers to determine the best way to test the code). For example, there could be a rule that 85 percent of the code you write needs to be checked with automated tests. In response, many software engineers—who had already tested the major risk areas—would waste time writing unnecessary test scripts just so they could conform to the 85 percent rule.

TOO MANY RULES LEAD TO TOO MANY LIES

The US Army requires company commanders to put their soldiers through 297 days of mandatory training each year, even though there are only 256 days available. A US Army War College study explains, "In the rush by higher headquarters to incorporate every good idea into training, the total number of training days required by all mandatory training directives literally exceeds the number of training days available." Yet commanders all report being compliant; noncompliance is not an option.

How can this be?

Retired army officers Leonard Wong and Stephen Gerras published a fascinating study titled *Lying to Ourselves: Dishonesty in the Army Profession* (Wong and Gerras 2015). Although the army officers interviewed wouldn't use the term "lie," they admitted that they routinely met required standards by getting "creative," by having one soldier take the online training repeatedly for everyone in the squad, by filling out forms and reports without actually doing the work. A term frequently used was, "we pencil whipped it."

Curiously, senior leadership seems okay with it. When one officer was asked if he believed the units under his command were submitting false data, he replied, "Sure, I used to do it when I was down there."

While fibbing on routine checklists may seem harmless or even amusing, it's less funny to hear it happens on the battlefield. Officers described falsifying inventory shortages to get additional equipment, falsifying poll site inspections during the Iraqi elections, falsifying readiness assessments of partner forces, and even losing track of large amounts of money intended to support local populations.

Wong and Gerras maintain that despite rampant dishonesty, military officers firmly cling to their self-identity as honest people who highly value integrity. Officers interviewed rationalized their dishonest actions by saying that nobody ever falsifies anything that's important. The question they had about so many of the demands put on them was, "You need this for why?"

Today army officers play this game from the top to the bottom. Rules are implemented in response to some crisis or demands from Congress or at the whim of a single general. Because it's impossible to comply with them all, soldiers "pencil whip" the information and move on. Those who collect the info pass the information up the chain of command knowing it's of questionable validity, and also believing it to be of no consequence.

The danger among troops—and in any organization—is that ethics can become a slippery slope. Every signature certifying something that isn't true, every checklist that is completed on paper only, every compliance claim that is false can cause them to become, in the words of the authors, "ethically numb." Bending the rules on the small things can lead over time to lying about bigger things: mistakes, actions, or achievements.

LIVING IN A "NO RULES" ORGANIZATION

Rules are a way for senior managers to micromanage from afar. Inevitably they disempower workers in the spirit of protecting against very low chances of risk or loss. Innovation, creativity, and risk-taking plunge. Morale drops as there is no sense of ownership; nobody likes to be micromanaged. Your ultimate goal is that your people make good decisions. To accomplish that, they must feel ownership of and accountability for those decisions. As individuals in your company think through decisions and prepare to answer for them, they develop that ownership mentality.

What you need is a framework that empowers your staff to make good decisions. So, ironically I'm offering up some rules that'll make the rest of the rules superfluous. Here are my "rule replacements."

RULE REPLACEMENT #1: HIRE THE RIGHT PEOPLE

Netflix is well known as one of the great success stories of the last two decades. Launched as a DVD-by-mail company in 1998, it now has thirty-five hundred employees and generates over $7 billion a year from eighty-one million subscribers to their online streaming service. Of course, the company doesn't just stream content—it also produces your favorite series like *Stranger Things*, *Orange Is the New Black*, and *The Crown*.

So what's the key to Netflix's sustained success? How does a company grow that fast, change business models so many times, and maintain a fanatical customer base?

Remember, rules are supposed to protect quality and consistency and profits as a company grows. Yet at Netflix, it's not the rules management put into place that account for their success, it's the absence of rules.

If you're familiar with the technology start-up scene, you've probably heard of the "Netflix Culture Deck" and its legendary influence. Facebook COO Sheryl Sandberg called this simple PowerPoint presentation "one of the most important documents to come out of Silicon Valley," and it's been viewed millions of times across the globe (Hass 2013).

In the famous presentation, Netflix leaders explain the traditional logic for rules and the short-term benefits of reducing mistakes. But the deck goes on to teach that over time, a process-focused culture drives out the high-performing employees that companies aim to keep. When the market shifts quickly due to new technology, competitors, or business models, rule-driven companies can't keep up and lose customers to competitors who adapt. In such an environment, slow-moving, rule-oriented companies grind "painfully into irrelevance" (Hastings 2009).

Netflix sums up its culture—and its competitive advantage—on slide one: Freedom and Responsibility.

Netflix asserts that a business should focus specifically on two things:

1. Invest in hiring high-performance employees.
2. Build and maintain a culture that rewards high performers and weeds out continuous, unimproved low performers.

Netflix leaders believe that responsible people—the people every company wants to hire—are not only worthy of freedom, they thrive on it. Creating an environment where these individuals are not inhibited by myriad rules allows them to become the best version of themselves.

Taking this belief to its literal meaning has spawned a series of human resource innovations that were previously unheard of. For example, consider the Netflix "unlimited vacation policy." Instead of establishing a formally tracked vacation policy, Netflix decided to allow salaried employees to take as much vacation time as they liked. (Hourly workers were given a more structured policy.) Certain guidelines were provided; for example, those working in accounting and finance were asked to be in the office during the beginning or end of a quarter. Additionally, anyone who wanted more than thirty days off in a row should meet with HR.

Netflix also resisted the urge to institute any type of formal travel and expense policy. According to former Netflix chief talent officer Patty McCord, "we decided to simply require adult-like behavior . . . The company's expense policy is five words long: 'Act in Netflix's best interests'" (McCord 2014). Employees were expected to spend company money as if it were their own, looking for opportunities to save when possible.

The results? The company saved money by allowing employees to book their own trips online, eliminating the need to pay a travel agent to do so.

Of course, there was also a learning curve. According to McCord, managers sometimes needed to speak with employees "who ate at lavish restaurants (meals that would have been fine for sales or recruiting, but not for eating alone or with a Netflix colleague)" (McCord 2014). Similarly, IT members could be prone to buying more gadgets than necessary. But McCord confirmed that the program was an overall success. It's still in effect today.

The true enabler of "no rules" at Netflix, the true enabler of their high-trust culture, was the fact that they did better hiring. In an article she penned for the January 2014 issue of *Harvard Business Review*, McCord sums up why this principle works so well:

If you're careful to hire people who will put the company's interests first, who understand and support the desire for a high-performance workplace, 97 percent of your employees will do the right thing. Most companies spend endless time and money writing and enforcing HR policies to deal with problems the other 3 percent might cause. Instead, we tried really hard to not hire those people, and we let them go if it turned out we'd made a hiring mistake (McCord 2014).

How can you apply this principle to your work environment? Ask yourself the following questions:

- How much more time and money should you invest into the hiring process?
- How are your managers being evaluated? For building great teams or for compliance with rules and getting all their reports submitted on time?
- What type of culture are you producing? Is it designed so high performers will thrive, or to protect against low performers?
- Are managers reluctant to let go of low performers? Why?

The higher the quality of your workforce, the less likely it is that you'll need rules. As McCord says, you should "hire, reward, and tolerate only fully formed adults."

RULE REPLACEMENT #2:
HOLD PEOPLE ACCOUNTABLE FOR RESULTS

Could accountability be more powerful than rules?

When I worked at Kenexa, I can remember my former partners and I trying very hard to increase "cross-selling" among our different divisions. Getting salespeople to share leads and clients across departments is a common problem in large organizations and notoriously hard to accomplish. We did all the usual stuff: held a "summit" to motivate everyone to cross-sell, trained each other on all our solutions, and mandated (i.e., made a rule) that every sales call include a secondary pitch of a cross-sell solution. Of course, nothing changed. Our frontline salespeople said they were pitching the "new" services, but the deal flow didn't change.

Then our CEO decided to make us—the business unit heads—truly accountable for cross-selling. He didn't put in new rules, didn't ask for more training, he did one simple thing. He told us, "I expect your teams to cross-sell other solutions, and 100 percent of your annual bonus is going to be tied to the amount you sell." One hundred percent! As an organization we thrived on variable pay formula (i.e., our fixed salary was relatively low and our bonus and commissions were relatively high), so that meant that about half our total annual pay would be tied to results from selling other people's stuff. I literally could have doubled the sales of my business unit, but if I didn't sell anybody else's solutions I would have gotten no bonus for that year. Suddenly everyone was cross-selling everything. Problem solved!

At the beginning of this chapter I described how my old CFO tried to control expenses by banning the purchase of sticky notes. Wouldn't it have been better to just set a quarterly office supply budget per person (by role) and hold people accountable for sticking to the budget? Even better of course would be to reward those who came in under their budget.

How can you pair accountability with coaching? Instead of a hard-and-fast no-beer rule, what if the CFO just flagged someone's manager when a meal reimbursement seemed out of line? Then a coaching conversation could take place. Maybe the high expense could be justified (e.g., "It was in Manhattan, I had worked all day and into the night skipping lunch and room service was the only option."). Or maybe not (e.g., "What, four beers at dinner is too many?"), but it would become a conversation that reinforces the expectations around professional behavior and expenses.

Instead of using rules, look for opportunities to build accountability by assigning ownership and consequences to your team's decision making.

RULE REPLACEMENT #3: GIVE GUIDELINES

Any talk about leading without rules would be incomplete without mentioning the Brazilian business visionary Ricardo Semler. Semler is the former CEO and president of Semco, which under his leadership grew from $4 million in revenue to over $160 million in about twenty years. All this without a mission statement, an org chart, or any written policies at all. And definitely without a rulebook.

So what was the key to Semco's success? One could point to various features of the radical industrial democracy that Semler ushered in during his tenure. But Semler himself epitomized it in his 2014 presentation at TED Global:

> We looked at it and we said, let's devolve to these people, let's give these people a company where we take away all the boarding school aspects of, this is when you arrive, this is how you dress, this is how you go to meetings, this is what you say, this is what you don't say, and let's see what's left. And so, the question we were asking was, how can we be taking care of people? People are the only thing we have (Semler 2014).

Power to the people.

Semler distributed that power in some unorthodox ways. For example, he let employees set their own salaries. Over twenty-five years ago, Semler put a computer in the company cafeteria that revealed how much revenue the company was taking in, the profit margins from that revenue, how much employees inside the company made, and how much employees in similar positions made. Armed with that information, the employee was then allowed to set his or her own salary. Did people pay themselves ridiculous amounts? No, it turned out that information and peer pressure kept pay at industry norms.

This is just one example of many—like Semco's refusal to track the amount of hours employees worked. And their freedom to take time off during the "workweek" to go see soccer matches. Or the fact that most meetings are voluntary, and that two seats at board meetings are open to the first employees to arrive. (Semler admitted that cleaning ladies sometimes voted on his board meetings. The result? They "kept us honest.")

Remember my example from Kenexa when the partners of the firm weren't allowed to expense a beer they had with dinner? Instead of a "no alcohol" rule, what if there was a guideline like, "When traveling for business and eating alone we try to keep the daily meal reimbursement to $35—and of course we are happy to split any savings with you if you should spend less than that."

What if instead of travel reimbursement rules there was a public spreadsheet that "racked and stacked" everyone's spending for the month? Imagine the power of peer pressure when you see most people are spending $25 per day on travel meals and you've been averaging $50 per day. What if the top 25 percent lowest spenders were celebrated or given gift cards as a thank you? Wouldn't expenses organically drop as everyone's sense of ownership also went up?

Rules by their nature send the message that you cannot be trusted to do the right thing, the smart thing. Rules are, well, rules—not to be broken. Guidelines are perceived as, and truly are, something very different. Guidelines are educational. They say, "Here's what we think is right in most circumstances, but do what's in the best interest of the company."

While you might be unwilling or unable to eliminate rules to the extent of Semco, how much more would your employees give you if you defaulted to trust? (Yes, an occasional bad apple [i.e., bad hire] will cause a problem that needs to be solved.) You need to ask questions like:

- What decisions am I willing to delegate to team members?
- What decisions do they wish I would delegate to them?
- What information do they need to have in order to make the right decision?
- How can we change our "policies" into "guidelines"?

As Semler wrote in a 1994 article for *Harvard Business Review*, "participation gives people control of their work, profit sharing gives them a reason to do it better, information tells them what's working and what isn't" (Semler 1994).

RULE REPLACEMENT #4:
STANDARDS AND VALUES INSTEAD OF RULES

When it comes to rules, remember, they take away the opportunity for employees to make a decision. It just so happens that my friend Jack Kloeber is one of the world's leading experts in decision analysis. A former army officer and pharmaceutical executive, Kloeber now leads the company Kromite, consulting with big companies about how to make strategic decisions objectively. So I asked him to explain "decision analysis" to a regular guy like me.

To my surprise, Kloeber said making decisions comes down to getting clear on your values. You need to analyze how the different choices you can make tie back to what matters most to you. Should you take the job offer that comes with both higher pay and a longer commute? You value both money and your time, of course. But how much would you value that specific increase in income? What is its value after taxes? What is the value of that raise compounded with interest over time? How would your life change from the additional income? What would you stop doing to add time to your commute? Stop watching Netflix, or stop tucking your daughter into bed at night? How can you meet both values better? Would your potential employer allow you to work from home one day a week? Would your spouse be able to work less since you have added income?

Earlier in the chapter I shared Coach K's disdain for rules. What does he do instead? As he wrote in his book *The Gold Standard*:

> In developing teams, I don't believe in rules. I believe in standards. Rules don't promote teamwork, standards do. Rules are issued by a leader to a group . . . When something is presented as a rule, you can't own it. You can't live it. Standards, on the other hand, are lived. This is what we do all the time. These are the things for which we hold one another accountable (Krzyzewski 2010).

More important, the standards come from the players, not the coach. Whether he's leading a team of NBA all-stars who are united as the USA Olympic team or young college athletes, Coach K sits down with the players and asks them to establish standards that everyone will abide by. In this way, they become the team's standards not the coach's rules, and they'll work far harder to hold one another accountable.

Dina Dwyer-Owens is cochairwoman of the Dwyer Group, a company with eleven franchise brands doing over a billion dollars in annual revenue. She credits strong values as a key to the success of the company. When I interviewed her on *The LEADx Leadership Show* she said that most companies pick some values and then ignore them, but at Dwyer they're used as tools.

> Make it become a way of life for you and your organization. We came up with these, what we call operationalized values, because they're not just respect, integrity, customer focus, and having fun. They're specific standards for how we expect ourselves to operate and how we expect each other to operate (Dwyer-Owens 2017).

She shared an example of an employee who in anger flipped off a coworker with her middle finger. Dwyer has a specific policy around communicating respectfully without profanity or sarcasm. The offending employee was counseled about her behavior, and a few months later she resigned on her own. Strong cultures tend to be self-reinforcing.

THE TAKEAWAY

Rules, policies, and procedures are implemented with the best of intentions to minimize risk (primarily financial loss). Because we as leaders can't be everywhere, we can't watch everyone, we implement rules to protect against wasteful spending, wasting time, and poor quality.

By protecting against the bad choices of the minority (about 3 percent according to Netflix experience) we are taking away the opportunity for 97 percent of our team members to reflect on company values, to develop decision-making skills, and to deepen their feelings of ownership and accountability. Instead of rules, leaders need to hire talent who can be trusted, make company values actionable, set guidelines, and be willing to coach those who make honest mistakes.

HOW MIGHT YOU APPLY THIS IF YOU'RE A:

MANAGER: Gather your team around a pizza and ask them variations on, "Hey, what rules and policies around here bother you the most? Which rules get in the way of you doing your job better?" Hear them out. Look for opportunities to replace rules with guidelines. When that's not possible, make sure they understand the intent behind the rule, why it's in place. Proactively manage up and ask your manager to explain the intent behind the rules and policies that you think are hurtful rather than helpful.

SALES PROFESSIONAL: A "no rules" philosophy in sales doesn't give license to break ethical boundaries; integrity with clients and your manager alike is paramount. Rather, you should strive to understand the why behind the rules that seem to get in your way. Yes, logging every prospective contact into your customer relationship management (CRM) system does take up your valuable time and brings you no value. But does tracking all that data across the entire sales function help sales management to understand seasonality, trends, and effectiveness of different sales tactics? And for the rules without a good "why," commit to being a change agent. Make sure your manager—your manager's manager or even the CEO—knows how much time every policy and procedure is taking you. Let them know how many hours you are spending each week on winning deals and how many you are spending on administration.

SPORTS COACH: From dress codes to curfews, it is true that athletic teams have a long culture of rules. But is there a better way? Instead of rules, ask your team to come up with a list of standards, or a code of conduct, that will help them to be their best. Explain that the failing of one player is a failing that impacts the entire team; the players must hold one another accountable. Have the players nominate several team leaders who can help reprimand or punish players when needed. Realize that rules by definition are inflexible but standards are conditional. An appropriate response to a first-time minor infraction might be a warning from team leaders; a minor infraction from a player who has had ongoing behavior problems might require you—the coach—to mete out severe punishment. Be the disciplinarian when you must, but only as a last resort.

MILITARY OFFICER: From dress code and salutes to reflective belts and operational risk management the military has numerous rules to maintain discipline, effectiveness, safety, and tradition. They aren't going away anytime soon. But when it comes to training requirements that are impossible to meet, or meeting them would interfere with war readiness, commanders should delegate the authority to not complete the task to the lowest level possible.

PARENT: At the risk of sounding like one of those annoying parents, I have great kids. Three teenagers who have strong grades, excel in activities, are very polite, and have never missed a curfew. Of course, they've never actually had a curfew. I'm sure I just hit some kind of parent lottery but I will add that they were raised with very few rules. Even as toddlers it wasn't, "You can't pull Natalie's hair!" but more about values, "We don't hurt other people because . . ." Even now in a time of high school parties, rather than telling them they have to be home by a certain time it's a conversation. They tell me how important or not this party is to them, I remind them that I can't go to sleep until I know they're home safe, and I ask what time they'd like to come home. Usually the time they suggest is earlier than the time I would have set as a rule. And if they get home five or ten minutes late it's no big deal, there is no punishment because it wasn't a rule. It was a guideline.

Let me add that if my kids were making bad decisions repeatedly that were putting themselves or others at physical risk, or if they were wasting large sums of money, you betcha I'd have rules. But again, I'd do it carefully and selectively only after the conversations around values and decisions and impact were worked through. The more rules you set down, the more it becomes your home, not their home; your family, not their family. And that's a dangerous place to be.

Think about the rules you have for your children. Could you replace the "go to bed at nine o'clock" rule with a conversation about getting enough sleep, when it would be OK to stay up late and when it is not? Could you replace a "no drinking" rule with a conversation about the dangers of alcohol and how disappointed you would be if you found out they were drinking, but also talking about how they should call you with no fear of punishment rather than drink and drive?

INDIVIDUAL: Do you have personal rules and don't even realize it? To uncover them, think about what you never do, or always do. Maybe you never date anybody who supports a different political party than you. Maybe you always say yes when your boss asks you to stay late, even with no notice on a Friday night when you have plans. Maybe you always give money to charitable causes when you're asked.

Reflect on these types of patterns and ask, Is it because of a rule that has been explicitly or implicitly put out by your parents, or religion, or societal norms . . . or is it from your values? Have you reflected on your values and made a conscious decision? If so, good for you. If not, think about your recurring behaviors and beliefs. What are your automatic decisions? Are they holding you back? Unmask hidden rules that might be controlling you without you even knowing it.

"There's something important I need to ask you," billionaire Brad Kelley began. "Do you need to be liked?"

"Well, I want to be liked," answered his twenty-four-year-old employee Daniel Houghton.

"That's not what I asked."

Houghton answered again, "I don't *need* to be liked."

"Good. Needing to be liked is a problem."

And then Kelley made young Houghton the CEO of the iconic guidebook company Lonely Planet, which Kelley had just acquired at a fire sale price (Bethea 2014).

In the US version of the television mockumentary *The Office*, regional manager Michael Scott (played by Steve Carell) gives a very different answer to this question.

Do I need to be liked? Absolutely not. I like to be liked.
I enjoy being liked. I have to be liked. But it's not like a
compulsive need to be liked. Like my need to be praised
(*The Office* 2007).

For the first twenty years of my career, I was Michael Scott.
And this turns out to be my single greatest weakness as a leader.
Notice I use present tense. I'm a recovering people pleaser. It's
something I'll always need to manage, to be wary of.

I used to be the boss who couldn't just tell you that your
performance was falling short. Sam was a great guy who just
wasn't cut out to be the kind of hunter-salesperson I wanted. It
was just a bad fit for him. Six months without any sales and I
still hemmed and hawed in my coaching sessions. "How do you
think things are going, Sam?" "How can I support you better,
Sam?" "You know all of our reps need to be closing a hundred
thousand a month. What can we do to get you there?" When I
finally fired him, he was totally shocked and hurt.

Another time I let a simple tweak to the organizational
chart spiral into six months of distraction. It started when I
mentioned in a town hall meeting that I thought it was time we
reorganized to better handle our continued growth. That triggered a long stream of "got-a-minute" requests from every single
employee. From those who feared who their new boss might
be, to the bosses who wanted to build their empires, everybody
wanted to give me their two cents. If that wasn't bad enough,
after drafting up a new organizational chart, I met again with
most people in the company as I tried to make everyone happy
with the new plan. That might have been a valiant effort at
democracy, but it wasn't leadership. The distraction and time-
wasting that unfolded was horrific.

The flaw I regret most was that I used to be the boss who

never said anything bad about you, at least not to your face. People think you're a swell guy until they hear you talking about them through paper-thin walls (sorry, Jim, I still feel guilty about that twenty-five years later). The only thing that makes me feel a tiny bit better about this specific bad habit is that legendary executive coach Marshall Goldsmith admitted to also having this flaw in his book *What Got You Here Won't Get You There* (Goldsmith 2007).

WE ALL WANT TO BE LIKED

Everyone except people with severe psychological disorders has an inner need to be liked and accepted. Have you ever met anyone who would rather be disliked by everyone?

Maslow's hierarchy of needs is a well-accepted theory of the stages of human growth and development. After our physiological needs (e.g., air, food, water) and our safety needs are fulfilled, we have the need for interpersonal belonging (affiliation, acceptance, affection). Perhaps this is hardwired into our human DNA, or perhaps it's an evolutionary instinct; after all, if our fellow cavemen didn't like us, we could be voted out of the cave and become dinner for saber-toothed tigers.

Regardless of its origin, society places a high value on friendship and friendliness. As children we are told to share our toys, stop arguing, and don't pull Jenny's pigtail. As teens our emotional radar pings madly in the high school cafeteria. Tray in our hands, eyes darting. Which table should I sit at? Where are my friends? Will I be rejected if I sit with that group? Oh no, I'm sitting alone—I'm such a loser!

Being liked at work (i.e., having friends at work) is a very good thing and encouraged. Having a "best friend" at work is strongly correlated with high employee engagement (Gallup

2017). It's why so many companies—especially those crazy Silicon Valley start-ups—spend so much time on company parties, foosball tables, free beer Fridays, and other mixers. It's for fun, and it's for bonding.

SO WHAT'S THE PROBLEM?

So if a sense of belonging and approval is a basic human need and having friends at work is a good thing, what's wrong with the boss wanting to be friends with the people on her team?

The distinction is subtle but critical. In a friendship, your relationship isn't tied to anything other than the pleasure of the social interaction itself. When you're the boss, your relationship with a subordinate is about achieving specific goals. Whether that goal is closing a million-dollar sale, or finishing the new software module, or assembling a thousand smartphones, having an objective in your relationship changes everything.

If you're the boss, it's easy to say that you and your direct reports are "equals" or peers. "Hey, I'm just like all of you, I just have a different job." It's easy to believe that you're the same as your team members and your role is just to coach. But it's just not true.

Ben Simonton commanded several ships as a captain in the US Navy and then led thousands of people as an executive in the electric power generation industry. He told me in no uncertain terms:

> Boss as a friend? It is one of the worst mistakes a boss can make. Almost everything a boss does is opposite to what a friend does. Friends don't decide on pay raises, train, coach, or rank their friends. Friends never criticize or cor-

rect a friend. The two responsibilities are quite different (Simonton 2017).

Typically, the role of the manager includes the power to fire direct reports. Even if that power isn't consolidated in one person, the manager typically has vast influence over people's careers. You have the power over the performance review. You have the power over the bonus or the annual raise. You have the power to put in a good word to higher-ups, to give a great or just average recommendation for internal hiring. The bottom line is that while pure friends are equals, there is absolutely a power differential between managers and their direct reports, whether you want it to be that way or not. Needing to be liked can cause specific problems as you execute your duties as team leader.

DELAYED OR SKEWED DECISION MAKING

Only in Silicon Valley can you start a company, grow it into something huge, be worth over $2 billion, and still be seen as a loser. But that's exactly what numerous venture capitalists and industry insiders think of Yahoo cofounder Jerry Yang. They don't actually call him "loser" but they say the downfall of Yahoo is Yang's fault because he was "too nice." You know, the opposite of acknowledged a**holes like Steve Jobs, Steve Ballmer, and Jeff Bezos.

The thesis is that Yang should have laid off employees to save money, but he didn't because he was too nice. They say Yahoo was strategically confused; it should have been either a media company or a tech company, but Yang tried to be both because he couldn't make the hard decision that would have affected half the company. When Microsoft and Google came courting with huge buyout offers, he refused them, because he was too nice to do that to his employees.

Blaming a giant company's slow decline in a fast-moving tech industry with aggressive competitors seems like a bit of a stretch to me. But I think the logic of needing to be liked or loved impeding decision making is a valid concern.

As venture capitalist Mark Suster wrote in his analysis of Yang and Yahoo's demise,

> Tough decisions don't always make you friends. By default if it's a "tough" decision some people will think you made the wrong one. And when it means a change in somebody's power, money or stature—or canceling a project that somebody has poured 18 months of their lives into—you're not going to be popular. Bad leaders want to be loved too much and their companies (or countries) suffer (Suster 2010).

Suster goes on to rightly describe a big part of the job of a CEO, or any team leader, which is the allocation of resources. There is never enough to go around. As a CEO you have to divvy up budget and head count between sales and marketing and product development and service—and you have to play counselor and resolve their never-ending conflicts. As a team leader maybe your decisions aren't as dramatic but you have to allocate scarce resources all the same. Who gets the office with the window that just became available? IT sent over two new laptops but you have five sales reps. Who gets the new computers? Someone has to come in over the weekend to finish some work and nobody is volunteering. Who gets volunteered by you?

The potential problem for those who have a need to be liked—again I'm looking in the mirror as I say this—is that these types of decisions can be skewed by your personal feelings toward your "friends," or they take forever to make as you try to get everyone to come to the decision together.

TOUGH CONVERSATIONS THAT NEVER HAPPEN

Similar to making tough decisions, managers who have a compulsive need to be liked are notorious for putting off tough conversations. Whether it's giving someone constructive criticism or having to mediate a dispute between two employees, conflict avoidance only makes matters worse. Stress and tension rises and things are left to fester. Often, exceptional talent will actually leave a company with this type of dysfunctional culture.

If you are unsure about whether you're conflict-avoidant or not, consider these questions:

- How frequently do you give constructive feedback to your team members?
- Do you often give people the benefit of the doubt for substandard work? (*It was probably just an off day. Those typos won't happen again I'm sure.*)
- How long do you wait before calling two feuding team members into your office for a "sit-down"?
- When it comes to annual performance ratings, if you had to round a score up or down, which would you lean toward?
- How would you feel if you confronted one of your team members and in reaction she started crying? Or yelling in anger?

What if you could replace your need for approval with something more powerful and effective?

REALIZE YOU WILL NEVER BE LIKED BY EVERYONE

There's actually nothing wrong with needing to be liked, or even wanting to be liked. It's the need to be liked by everyone that's the problem.

In the past, I would give a speech and get thunderous applause at the end, but I'd dwell for days on that one guy in the third row who I saw actually fell asleep. I'd have a 360 survey done to evaluate my management effectiveness and I'd get nine positive comments and one negative comment. *I wonder who said that? That's so not true!* I'd read my 100+ positive book reviews on Amazon but be really hurt by the two one-star reviews people would write. I'd want to argue back with them or explain to Amazon why they should take down the false reviews.

Think about so many greats: Martin Luther King, Gandhi, Jesus. All had haters. They knew that doing the right thing wouldn't necessarily be the popular thing. Did you know that even Mother Teresa has haters? Mother Teresa! Indeed there are many who have accused her of providing unnecessarily reckless medical care (e.g., not sterilizing needles or isolating patients with tuberculosis). Others claim she was secretly baptizing (i.e., converting) Muslims and Hindus right before they died. Still others take umbrage with her close relationship with Albanian dictator, and Stalin wannabe, Enver Hoxha (Wikipedia n.d.).

You have to realize that you will never get everybody to love or like you. You have to move from needing to be liked by everyone to being happy when enough people like you.

Can you reframe a need to be liked by everyone with a need to be loved by just a few people? Does your spouse love you? Do your kids love you? Do your parents love you? Do you have a few friends to go shopping or watch the game with? That's enough! That's all you need.

IT'S NOT ABOUT YOU

Do you think being everyone's friend is "the right way" to treat people? Do you think if people like you it's a sign that you're a good boss? Maybe you need to reframe it and realize that needing people to like you is about you; it's a selfish act.

Michael Hillan is owner and principal at DriveTrain Learning and, like me, part of his leadership journey was coming to terms with his need to be liked. He explained in an interview:

> I grew up wanting everyone to like me, and feeling very ashamed if someone didn't. I took it as a personal challenge to get them to like me without really seeking to understand why we may have been at odds. It was all my agenda to be liked instead of seeking to understand.
>
> It was this pivot—seeking to understand first—that allowed me to shift frames to seeking respect from my team members and colleagues. When seeking to understand the other's perspective, needs, and drives, a leader gains significant insight into how that person likes to be led. In my experience, this then facilitates likability as well, particularly if the leader is welcoming to that aspect of a relationship (Hillan 2017).

Do football players need the head coach to be their friend? Or do they need the coach to push them, to challenge them, to correct them in order to make them better? Helping others to become the best they can be—even if they don't like it—that is the selfless act.

REPLACE YOUR NEED TO BE LIKED
WITH THE NEED TO LEAD RIGHT

If you haven't already done this, now is a good time to reflect on what you think makes a great leader. What are your leadership values? What do you hope for in those who lead you? What is your leadership truth?

Some of what I value: transparency, authenticity, treating people fairly, making decisions objectively, caring for my team members. Those are the standards that I'll measure myself against, not whether or not the people at work like me. I can still care about people even if they don't return it.

If you are living your values . . . if you are leading your values . . . then let other people think whatever they want. As Super Bowl champion Gary Brackett once told me, "What other people think of me is none of my business" (Brackett 2017). You don't have to be a jerk. But you need to respect yourself above all else. Don't worry about people second-guessing your decision or gossiping about you behind your back. Over time, leading consistently based on values, you may not be everyone's friend but you'll certainly have earned their respect.

TOUGH AND TENDER

Doug Conant is one of the CEO leaders I admire most. When he joined the Campbell Soup Company in 2000, the company was experiencing declining sales, had lost 54 percent of its market value, and Conant was told that their employee engagement levels were the worst ever seen among the Fortune 500.

Most turnaround CEOs focus on bold moves like selling off divisions, or reorganizing the entire company. But what was at the core of Conant's turnaround plan? As he told one business reporter, "To win in the marketplace . . . you must first win in the workplace. I'm obsessed with keeping employee engagement front and center." And quarter after quarter, year after year, Conant made sure that employee engagement was one of Campbell's top initiatives (Gallup 2010).

By 2009, Campbell's had achieved an astounding 23-to-1 engaged-to-disengaged employee ratio. More important, in the decade that saw the S&P 500 stocks lose 10 percent of their value, Campbell's stock actually increased by 30 percent.

How can you drive tremendous financial gains in your company while simultaneously focusing on employee engagement? Conant summarizes his leadership philosophy in a single phrase, "Be tough-minded on standards, and tenderhearted on people."

Most managers think they have to be a hard-nosed results-driving autocrat, or a kind people-focused servant. Conant reminds people of the power of "and." It doesn't have to be one or the other. You can be tough and tender at the same time. Be clear with your expectations and hold people accountable. If Laura knows that salespeople have a quota of $50,000 in revenue each month, you can still care about her as a person as you coach her through her shortfalls and, if necessary, eventually let her go. You can be kind, compassionate, and supportive while being rigid about results.

THE TAKEAWAY

Management guru Peter Drucker had it right when he said, "Effective leadership is not about making speeches or being liked; leadership is defined by results, not attributes." Striving to be liked may feel good in the short term, but it's a recipe for disaster in the long term. Instead, you should try to be friendly, without striving to be friends. You should try to be likable, without caring whether you are liked. You should care for your colleagues and also maintain the highest standards.

HOW MIGHT YOU APPLY THIS IF YOU'RE A:

MANAGER: It's time for honest introspection. Have you been withholding direct feedback or delaying tough decisions? Remember that your team needs a leader, not another friend. You are in a unique position to help employees to improve their performance, which will help their careers. If you need to, remind everyone of the standards—your expectations—during your next team meeting. Then actively look for ways to hold people accountable.

SALES PROFESSIONAL: As a sales professional do you need your clients to like you? Many go into sales because they like people, they're relators, and they thrive on social interactions. And it's true, all else being equal, people would rather buy from people they like. But what about the tough conversations? Are you too quick to drop your price just to keep the client happy? Are you slow to ask for a change order even though the client clearly changed the specs? Realize you are a sales professional, not an order taker. Your first loyalty is to your company. Think about your best clients. Do you need to rein them in in any way? Do you need to reestablish what defines a win-win relationship?

SPORTS COACH: In my experience most coaches err on the side of the screaming intimidator, but I've had a few who seemed to want to be everyone's friend. Are you reluctant to address the bad behavior of your star players? Are you sure you're choosing the starting lineup based on skill and not on favoritism? Use the beginning of each season to have the players come up with behavior standards for the year. With your team captains, enforce those standards regardless of how you feel personally about your players.

MILITARY OFFICER: I've long been curious about friendship and leadership in the military. I know that soldiers, sailors, and marines who serve together often form bonds that are more like family than even friendship. Yet what happens when one "brother" gets promoted and the other doesn't? I reached out to my friend, retired US Marine Corps colonel John Boggs, to give me insights. He said, "The key is the mutual respect. The new junior, if you will, is very conscious of the new relationship and maintains respect for the rank as well as respect for the friendship. The new senior does the same. The 'first name' relationship is put in its place for the proper time and place. I once had to severely chastise a friend who was my junior. Once the day was done, it was just the two of us; I popped my head into his office and asked, 'What time are we going for that beer?'"

PARENT: Your child can also be your friend, but remind them, and yourself, that you need to be a parent first. Do you let them eat whatever they want, whenever they want, so that they'll like you? Do you let them watch YouTube all night instead of doing their homework because you don't want them to get mad at you? Realize that making your kids happy now doesn't necessarily prepare them to deal with the real world as adults. Do they need another friend, or a strong parent? Perhaps it's time to chat about family standards and explain that everyone needs to recommit to honoring them.

INDIVIDUAL: Even as an individual, you can practice self-leadership. And individuals are also leaders—influencers—of those around them. It's been said that we teach others how to treat us. Do you need people to like you so badly that you let them treat you poorly? Does your fear of confrontation prevent you from standing up for your beliefs? Are you always the one compromising? Realize that true friends will like you—even love you—despite the disagreements, fights, or decision as to where to go for dinner tonight. The next time you think some-one is treating you badly, remember your pride and your values, and address the situation.

Tom Coughlin led the New York Giants for twelve years. When he joined the team in 2004, he was known as a strict disciplinarian and was called (certainly only behind his back) "Tom Tyrant" and "Colonel Coughlin." Among his more unusual rules was "Coughlin Time," which stated that unless you arrived five minutes early to a meeting, you were late. So players who showed up three minutes early were actually fined from $500 to $1,000 for being "late." Star players like defensive lineman Michael Strahan and running back Tiki Barber did little to hide their hatred of their new coach.

As Coughlin himself explained, in his book *Earn the Right to Win*, "I had learned the art of communication from my parents, and from the nuns in elementary school, who basically communicated with a pointer to your knuckles." After a dismal losing season in 2006, Coughlin was told by team management that he had to change or go. To everyone's surprise, he changed. While he still maintained unusually strict standards, he worked hard to be more positive, to control his temper, and to show his players that he actually cared about them (Coughlin 2014).

And it worked. Year after year Coughlin continued his personal transformation and improved his relationship with the Giants' players. It culminated in 2012 before the Super Bowl with his pregame speech. He said, "You guys have taught us what love really is. When you put it on the line the way you do every Sunday, when your ass is up against the wall, you have taught us what love really is. And I am man enough to tell you guys that I love you, and these guys [the coaches] all love you" (Coughlin 2014).

The Giants beat the New England Patriots in Super Bowl XLVI and Coughlin's transformation was complete. His love wasn't unrequited. His onetime rival Strahan would eventually pen the foreword to Coughlin's book. Strahan wrote, "From a cold and distant figure, he became the man none of us wanted to disappoint . . . I tell people proudly that I love the man" (Coughlin 2014).

THE L WORD

Should a leader love her followers?

You might think the answer is no; after all, we did just agree in an earlier chapter that we should not be friends with our direct reports. So what exactly am I talking about when I say we need to lead with love?

It has been said that Eskimos have dozens of words for snow, and it turns out the ancient Greeks had at least six different words for love. Their language captured the distinction between the sexual chemistry between young adults, the deep understanding between long-married couples, close friendships, emotions between parents and children, and more.

The love I'm referring to the Greeks called "agape" (*agápē*) or a selfless love of everyone. The concept of universal love is an anchor of many world religions. Christians speak of the unconditional love of God and Jesus for all mankind. Often quoted is the book of Peter, "Above all, love each other deeply, because love covers over a multitude of sins." And from the book of Matthew, "Love your neighbor as you love yourself." In Buddhism, *mettā* is a term that means "loving-kindness" toward other people and it is one of the four key Buddhist virtues.

With agape love you don't love someone for who they are, or for what they do, or for how they make you feel. You love them unconditionally as a human. You have a genuine heartfelt concern and care for their well-being. You love each team member as an individual (an individual who has a life outside of work), not as a soulless cog in your production machine.

Dr. Sigal Barsade, a professor of management at the Wharton School of the University of Pennsylvania, studies something called "companionate love." She defines companionate love as an "other focused" affection and sensitivity to other people (Barsade & O'Neill 2014). It's a type of love that expresses itself as affection, caring, compassion, and tenderness. Stuff that won't get you into trouble with HR.

I know what you're thinking. *Yeah, but Kevin, Jesus, and Buddha never had to deal with Pat who shows up late every day and I know is stealing people's lunches out of the fridge!* You might find this idea tough to swallow. Love the people who whine, and moan, and don't do their job? Love the people who don't make a new pot of coffee when they pour the last cup? Love the people who drive you crazy half the time?

I gained a fuller understanding of the capacity to love from none other than legendary basketball coach John Wooden. Wooden was notorious as a hard-driving leader who had rules about how players were to put on their socks, tie their shoes, trim their fingernails, and cut their hair (unlike Coughlin version 1.0, Wooden always explained the logic behind these rules). Wooden was not a warm and fuzzy guy. But in his book *Wooden on Leadership,* he devotes an entire chapter to love and it opens with, "I will not like you all the same, but I will love you all the same" (Wooden 2005). This is something that doesn't come easy to me. But I remind myself of it all the time. Whether I like you, and whether you like me, is irrelevant. In our daily interactions I will lead with love. Who said leadership is easy?

WHY LEADERS DON'T LOVE

"It is better to be feared than loved" has been the prevailing leadership wisdom for five hundred years, ever since an Italian diplomat penned *The Prince* in 1513. Traditional wisdom—and many modern managers—argues that you can't get close or personal with your team members because doing so:

- undermines respect in the boss-worker relationship,
- prevents maintaining objectivity, and
- makes it more difficult to reprimand or fire others.

Although I never had any formal management training, advice and messages I received from elders include:

- "Leadership is acting."
- "You can try to be kind to your employees, but they'll just be ungrateful."
- "Productivity is higher if they think they might be fired."

You were probably raised on similar advice. When I posed the question on LinkedIn, dozens of people shared the advice they received to put up walls between themselves and those they lead. Paul Maskill shared that he was told, "If you give them too much praise, they'll get complacent and take what they learned on your dime to help someone else grow their business."

And Jamie Alford said:

Early on in my career, I had a manager tell me if I was too friendly with my team they would try to "pull things over on me." That to be effective, I needed to be distant and "for the love of God, Jamie, stop being so nice. You make yourself seem like the girl who gets the coffee." That "advice" haunted me for years. I tried that manager's advice out and, honestly, that was the worst period of my career. I felt horrible, not to mention not very effective. What is wrong with pouring coffee anyway? I find true leadership is leading with your heart.

Taking this advice to heart, or should I say, making sure they stay closed-hearted, many managers put up metaphorical walls. They might avoid topics of conversation related to family or personal interests; they never speak of their own lives outside the office. They stay out of office pools, fantasy leagues, or other games. They decline invitations to eat lunch with team members.

Well, I'll see your five-hundred-year-old Machiavellian advice and raise you with twenty-five-hundred-year-old advice from Lao Tzu. He preached that the best leader is the one who helps people so that eventually they don't need him. And historically, the weight of Machiavelli's recommendation lightens considerably when you realize that his full sentence was, "It is better to be feared than loved, if you cannot be both" (emphasis mine).

Indeed, it's far easier to be a manager of tasks than a leader of people. It's easier to control than to love. It's easier to direct than to coach. But what is expeditious isn't what will get you results over the long term.

BENEFITS OF LEADING WITH LOVE

Research and our own experiences indicate that while leadership based on fear may be the norm, and can be motivating, it doesn't actually lead to good long-term results. Fear crushes creativity, innovation, and new ideas. Fear shuts down communication. When we fear, we are more likely to sweep problems under the rug. Fear contributes to stress, blocks engagement, and causes us to look for a new job. Love is the opposite of fear.

Dr. Barsade's research into "companionate love" includes a sixteen-month-long study of outcomes in a long-term health care facility, conducted with colleague Olivia O'Neill, an assistant professor of management at George Mason University. They used outside raters, family members, the employees, and patients themselves to report on emotional culture and signs of caring and compassion. A key finding was that departments that had higher cultures of love also had lower levels of employee absenteeism and burnout. Conversely these same departments showed higher levels of employee satisfaction and teamwork. There was also a strong positive correlation between love and patient quality of life. When it came to actual health outcomes, the data was mixed. A culture of love correlated to a reduction in emergency room visits, but showed no correlation to bedsores or weight gain. Building on this initial research, Barsade and O'Neill launched a more ambitious study, this time with over three thousand employees working in seven different industries. The results were the same, love correlated to satisfaction, engagement, and accountability (Barsade and O'Neill 2014).

The Gallup Organization has conducted numerous research studies showing the links between employee engagement and business results. Based on survey results from more than twenty-five million employees, the Gallup Organization has identified twelve key elements that drive employee engagement. Notable is question number five in their "Q12 Survey," which states, "My supervisor or someone at work cares about me." This caring question and the other eleven items are shown to affect employee turnover, safety, shrinkage, productivity, customer satisfaction, and even profitability (Harter et al. n.d.).

When we work in a place with an abundance of love—love from our peers and love from our leader—we feel safe. And safety and trust are the foundations for feeling emotionally connected to our work, for the release of discretionary effort, and for loyalty. It is notable that two giants in the field of leadership development, James Kouzes and Barry Posner, conclude the sixth edition of *The Leadership Challenge* with these words, "The best-kept secret of successful leaders is love: staying in love with leading, with the people who do the work . . . Leadership is not an affair of the head. Leadership is an affair of the heart" (Kouzes and Posner 2017).

So how do we lead with love? How can we nurture the emotion and love as a verb? When Professor Barsade went to measure companionate love in the workplace, she looked for signs of affection, caring, compassion, and tenderness.

LET YOURSELF LOVE

I believe that caring for other people is our natural state. Whether it's innate or part of learned response to thriving in a tribe, feeling a communal love for others is the natural state. So why is it so hard to do? Why don't we more readily feel love for our colleagues at work? Either through lessons or experience we learn that it's easier and less painful if we withhold our feelings. Men especially can become inhibited emotionally when they're raised with parental and societal messages of "big boys don't cry" and that tough guys are stoic.

You may have also learned to distance yourself from your followers because of the pain you felt in the past when you had to fire them, or reprimand them. Perhaps it hurt when you caught someone you were close to at work gossiping about you, or maneuvering to beat you out on that promotion. Maybe colleagues have lied to you or even stolen from you. I still feel hurt when I think about Mike betraying my trust, Rudy lying about me after I left the firm, close employees who left me for another company.

To begin loving your colleagues, you don't do anything, you stop doing things. Stop avoiding the pain associated with betrayal, disappointment, or loss. I know that in the future, people I lead—people I care about—will steal, lie, cheat, and leave. But I remember that nobody is perfect; past employees acted in a way that they thought was best for them (they weren't trying to hurt me). These days I choose to focus on all the things they did for me and the company, how their gifts outweigh their mistakes. I forgive them.

It might help to reassociate in your mind what it means to be tough. Who are your models for toughness and strength? Personally, the toughest people I know—Marine Corp officers, Navy SEALs, NFL football players—all lead with love.

At the time I'm writing this the hottest name in college football coaching is Tom Herman. He had an amazing run as head coach at the University of Houston and is about to begin his first season leading the Texas Longhorns team at the University of Texas at Austin. Herman has repeatedly made headlines by, of all things, kissing his male players before each football game. His ritual includes a full embrace, a peck on the cheek or neck, and a few words of encouragement for every player. Even the *New York Times* covered Herman with the headline, "Houston's Coach Pecks Away at Football's Macho Culture, a Kiss at a Time" (Tracy 2016). As he explained in the article, "How do you motivate a human being . . . love and fear. And to me, love wins every time."

I'm not advocating physical contact at work, but if tough male gladiators can show their love for each other surely you can find ways to show that you care too. So let's begin . . .

YOU HAD ME AT HELLO

Paul Marciano is an executive coach who has worked with hundreds of executives. A standard practice of coaches is to implement some form of a 360 survey, in which one's boss, peers, and direct reports all critique you anonymously. Over lunch one day I was shocked when Paul told me that one of the most common complaints he sees is some form of, "He walks past my cube every single day and has never once said, 'Good morning.'"

Are there that many bosses who don't say good morning? And do people really notice?

As I've conducted my own employee research, indeed this comes up as one of the most common complaints. In fact, even more common than the complaint about morning greetings is the complaint, "Whenever we pass in the hall he doesn't even make eye contact!" When I explore the problem with this, many people attach meaning to this behavior. I've heard, "He thinks he's better than everyone else." And, "He acts like I don't even exist."

I think it's this latter comment that gets to the root of the issue. While most of us don't think much about our simple hellos, in the past greetings have meant much more. The common Hindu greeting "Namaste" has a literal meaning of "I bow to you" but an implied meaning of "I bow to the divine in you" (Wikipedia n.d.). Management thought leader Peter de Jager has written about the need—in many societies—for identity. He writes:

> The Zulu greeting, "Sawubona" means "I see you" and the response "Ngikhona" means "I am here." As always when translating from one language to another, crucial subtleties are lost. Inherent in the Zulu greeting and our grateful response, is the sense that until you saw me, I didn't exist. By recognizing me, you brought me into existence. A Zulu folk saying clarifies this, "Umuntu ngumuntu nagabantu," meaning "A person is a person because of other people" (de Jager 2003).

This concept was actually used in James Cameron's movie *Avatar.* On the alien world of Pandora, the Na'vi species say "I see you" as a greeting with a deeper meaning. Similar to the Zulu tradition, Cameron has described the greeting as expressing "that we are all connected to each other as human beings" (Oprah.com 2010).

If you're thinking, *I show them I care when I hand them their paycheck,* I get it. I used to be the guy that walked past everyone in the hallway without acknowledging them. It wasn't because I didn't care; it wasn't because I thought I was better than them. It was because I was a type A driver who was late for my next call, my next meeting, and my next deadline. I was just inside my own head thinking about work. I figured, I already said hello on Monday of this week, why do I need to say it over again?

While saying hello in the hallway wasn't important to me, I've learned acknowledgments are vital to others. I now consider making eye contact and giving a smile when I pass people by as a small part of leading with love. The eye contact is the key. It's a moment in time when you are connecting with a team member. There is no doubt about it. It may not be verbal, but you are saying, "I see you."

THE LITTLE THINGS

I can picture her clearly. Boca Raton, Florida, hotel ballroom. I was giving a speech to a few hundred HR professionals. She was waving her arm back like she was trying to hail a cab. I had asked a string of questions, "Think about the worst boss you ever had. What did she do that made her so bad? What didn't he do that made him so bad?" The question was meant to be rhetorical. But there she was (standing now!) waving her arm. I had no choice but to call on her.

"He didn't know my kids' names."

At first I wasn't sure I heard her right. *Her kids' names?* "Can you say that again?" I asked.

"I worked for him for ten years, and he didn't even know the names of my children."

And the audience supported her with vigorous applause. In fact, she got more applause than I did at the end of my speech!

Since that day I've looked into this issue and it comes up quite a bit. In my own research and in discussions with numerous executive coaches, I've come to learn that common complaints about bosses are: *They don't know the name of my spouse, or my children. They don't know that I'm taking care of a parent with Alzheimer's. They don't know that I ran a marathon.*

Some people have the misconception that loving your employees is about baring your soul, and letting them cry on your shoulder, or doing trust falls. It's not. People are looking for signs that you know they exist, that they matter, and that you care. It's the little things each day, or each week. Things like:

- On Friday do you ask team members what they have planned for the weekend?
- On Monday morning do you ask them how their weekend was? (Bonus points if you ask specifically about the things they told you on Friday.)
- Do you know the names of their spouse and children?
- Do you know if they have any special hobbies or activities they enjoy?
- What type of movies do they enjoy? What kind of books do they enjoy?
- Do you acknowledge their birthdays? Their work anniversaries?

SHAPE THEIR FUTURE

Another easy way to show you care about each of your team members is to hold one-on-one career-path meetings at least every six months. In my previous books I've described how growth, recognition, and trust are the three primary drivers of engagement. When it comes to growth, we want to be doing challenging work, learning and advancing in our careers. With your coaching hat on, you can help boost them up the next rung on their career ladder.

Some managers are reluctant to fully embrace the development and career progression of their team members because they are afraid of losing them. And indeed, it's easier than ever before to leave one company and join another. People think it's a generational thing, but it's not. It's just that all the friction has gone out of the process. You can start your own company in a day for a few dollars. It doesn't even seem weird anymore if you work from home. Instead of reading through the weekly Help Wanted section of your local newspaper, you can type in specific search terms and scour thousands of jobs around the world. And headhunters flip it around and can find you easily, too.

When I interviewed executive coach and author of *Fiercely Loyal*, Dov Baron, he explained the ironic truth, especially if you want to retain millennials. He told me, "Don't allow them to get bored. Millennials love to learn." You will actually keep your talented people longer, the longer you get them ready for their next step. And what was Baron's reaction when his top employee did leave him? Baron said, "When he left us at five years, he opened a company and we were his first customer" (Baron 2017).

When you hold career-path meetings with your direct reports, they don't have to be an official HR-driven event. Rather, grab a cup of coffee or go out for pizza and have an informal conversation. "Aanya, it's been a while since we chatted about your career goals. Do you still want to be a . . ." Topics to ask about could include:

- Where would you like to be in one year, three years, five years . . . ?
- Do you think you accomplish the goals in this organization? Why or why not?
- What do you need to learn to achieve your goals?
- Who do you need to know to achieve your goals?
- What experiences do you need to have to achieve your goals?

WAYS TO EXPRESS LOVE

When it comes to love—whether at work or in your personal life—a helpful concept is to realize and remember that people can express and receive love in different ways. Dr. Gary Chapman, author of *The Five Love Languages* (Chapman 2015), believes that love can be expressed as:

- words of affirmation
- quality time
- gifts
- favors
- physical touch

He also believes that while we all express and receive all these forms of love, most of us have a preferred or dominant style.

I don't really know if there are five love languages or ten or only four, but I think the concept is very important. Different people express love in different ways. How much angst from childhood issues would vanish if people understood this concept? My own father didn't often say the words *I love you*. But when I think back on my childhood, I have great memories of him reading to me at bedtime, playing board games with me and my friends, taking me to the batting cages in a hopeless attempt to reduce the odds of me striking out; and I still treasure the Swiss army knife and the autographed baseball that he gave me over thirty years ago. All these things are expressions of love.

When it comes to words of affirmation, compliments and thank-yous are powerful, easy to implement, and low cost. In the last hour alone, I said "Great catch!" to Tara when she found and fixed an error I made in a document, and I sent a message to Vania saying, "Hey, nice webinar graphic for LinkedIn!" These are sincere. When it comes to positive feedback, I follow the TSA motto, "If you see something, say something."

The research on gratitude at work is quite shocking. In a study funded by the John Templeton Foundation, 81 percent of respondents said they'd work harder if their manager was more grateful. And yet 74 percent of these same people say they never express gratitude to their boss. While a sincere "thank you" goes a long way to making team members feel cared about and appreciated, a handwritten thank-you note goes even further. Former Campbell's Soup CEO Doug Conant is legendary for writing ten to twenty thank-you notes every single day; it's estimated that he sent thirty thousand thank-you notes during his decade at Campbell's. Everybody keeps those notes from their boss, either tacked up on their cube wall or in a special folder at home.

You might think you're already spending enough time with your team members, but how often do you do one-on-ones? When was the last time you took someone to lunch just to connect? For your family, when was the last time you went on a date night, or had a Mommy-Daughter day? Quality time can be especially powerful when you skip levels in an organization. Retired Marine Corps general James "Mad Dog" Mattis, currently serving as secretary of defense, is beloved by Marines partly because he spent so much time talking to privates and corporals (often while on the front lines of combat) during his four decades of service.

Love in the form of gifts doesn't have to be expensive. Random and thoughtful matter more than the cost. What pleases you more, a dozen roses on Valentine's Day or a spring bouquet just because? As a boss I've given gifts of movie tickets, books, restaurant gift cards, days off from work, and unasked-for cups of coffee. And if you really want to make an impact, get an age-appropriate gift for someone's kid.

Acts of service—doing someone a favor—is another one of Chapman's love languages. I would actually argue that if you're leading right, almost everything you do is an act of service. The concept of leadership as service goes back thousands of years, but it was Robert Greenleaf who coined the modern-day term "servant leadership." It's a model where we are servants first. We become leaders not out of a desire for power or wealth but rather as an expression of wanting to support those on our teams. More practically, we as leaders can help our colleagues on a tough task, cover their shifts, and keep them informed of important information.

When it comes to physical touch, there is probably no more charged "love language" in the workplace. Too many of us have experienced or witnessed hugs that went on too long or inappropriate and creepy shoulder massages. But we can all feel comfortable with a firm handshake, a high five, or gentle fist bump. And of course at home, go ahead and hug and kiss your kids. The more the better.

THE TAKEAWAY

Too often we withhold our feelings at work due to our own insecurities, or because we were taught that managers need to stay aloof to remain objective. Great leaders know that caring for their people is a secret to activating employee engagement. You don't have to even like them but you can still love them. People perform better and stay longer when they know you care.

HOW MIGHT YOU APPLY THIS IF YOU'RE A:

MANAGER: Forget about the past; separate liking your colleagues from loving your colleagues. Commit to greeting your team members in the morning and acknowledge them as you pass in the hall. Learn the names of their family members. Hold informal career-path meetings with each of your directs—what are their goals, how might you help them to get there? Catch people doing things right and show your appreciation.

SALES PROFESSIONAL: Do you think your customers and clients want you to care—or even to love—them? I'm sure they don't expect it, but they sure would like it. If you love them, they'll trust that you are going to do what's right by them. You would never recommend something that wasn't truly in their best interest. How can you show them that you care? Inquire about their kids and outside interests. Instead of giving gifts that are really just advertisements for your company (e.g., logo'd pens and desk calendars), give appropriate gifts that are about them. Ask them about their career plans. If you are the one who helps them to advance, they'll be certain to make a smooth transition to their replacement, and they may give you new business when they settle into their new role.

SPORTS COACH: You are a seminal figure in the lives of your players. You teach them how to win in sports, and you can teach them how to win in life. Remember the lessons of Wooden, Coughlin, and Herman. You don't have to like all your players to love them all. What's going on in your players' lives off the practice field? The next time your star player makes a mistake say, "I know you feel badly, but what are you going to do next. Are you going to keep that mistake with you, or show everyone out here that you are focused and determined?"

MILITARY OFFICER: What opportunities do you have to "lead from the front"? Perhaps you can cover a junior's duty or work beside her. Perhaps you can reinforce good safety practices. Do you take a genuine interest in your troops (or sailors, airmen, or marines)? Inquire about family members, asking whether they have what they need. How do you treat even the most junior personnel?

PARENT: While loving our kids comes naturally, often expressing that love does not. It starts easily hugging and kissing our babies and toddlers, but sometimes fades as our kids turn into rebellious teens and on into adulthood. Tell your kids you love them. Even when you don't like them (they can really be such selfish ungrateful snots, can't they?), love them. Make a big deal about greeting them each day, whether it's when they stumble out of bed in the morning or you stumble into the house after a day of work. Catch them doing things right and show your appreciation. Get their favorite snack when they are studying for a big exam. Make sure you know who their best friends are at school. Ask them what they are happiest about and what is stressing them out. Let them know you will always have their back.

INDIVIDUAL: Who do you love? Who are the friends, family members, and colleagues you care about most in life? Think about how you can let them know. Say "thank you" or send a thank-you card to colleagues in the office. Offer to babysit your friends' kids for a few hours so the couple can have a date night. Send a handwritten card to your minister and let her know how much you enjoyed the sermon this week. Buy some flowers for a neighbor, just because.

Hang around with me for even a little while and you'll see that I'm obsessed with time. On the bottom of my computer monitor—I'm glancing at it as I type this sentence—is a sticker that says "1440." It's a constant reminder that there are 1,440 minutes in a day, and once they're gone, they're never coming back. Also on my desk is an unusual little clock. Officially called a Time Timer, its red dial spins down the time, a great visual reminder of how many minutes are left in a work sprint. I'm notoriously cheap and not into art but when I sold my last company, I splurged on a painting by Peter Tunney called *The Time Is Always Now*. It cost me as much as a small automobile. And of course I took a couple years of my life to study the habits of high achievers and wrote a book about their extreme productivity habits.

At first I wasn't sure I was going to include this chapter in this book. My imaginary critics, always whispering in my head, *This isn't a time-management book. Stay focused!* Yet, when I reflect on the most successful leaders, they stand out because of their ability to lead great teams, and to get sh*t done. Am I biased? Perhaps. But if you're a leadership junkie like I am, you can't help but notice how many great leaders are obsessed with time. You begin to have an ear for it, picking up on unusual phrases they use that reference time or productivity.

GREAT LEADERS FOCUS ON MINUTES

Mike Krzyzewski is one of the greatest basketball coaches of all time. Coach K has led the Duke University Blue Devils men's basketball team for almost four decades. He's also been head coach, or assistant coach, to fourteen different USA Basketball teams, which have won ten gold medals. In his book, *The Gold Standard: Building a World-Class Team*, he shares leadership secrets he used to take individual stars and turn them into a team larger than themselves. The book begins with a section titled, "Team Building in Time and Moments" (emphasis mine). He writes:

> When you are given the responsibility of building a team, you must make time for certain things. Time to form relationships. Time to establish standards. Time to get motivated . . . Leaders are responsible for ensuring that you spend both the necessary quantity and quality of time to get the job done and for making certain that no time is wasted (Krzyzewski 2010).

Every single one of Coach K's book chapters begins with the word *Time* (e.g., "Time to Choose Your People," "Time to Gain Perspective," "Time to Form Relationships"). He even concludes his book reminding the reader to take time to celebrate.

Another basketball coaching legend, John Wooden, dedicated an entire chapter in his book *Wooden on Leadership* to time mastery. He writes,

> A leader must be skillful—a master—in using time productively and teaching others to do the same. Your skill in doing this directly impacts on the ability of your organization to compete—even survive . . . I had a fetish about using time efficiently—not wasting it . . . carefully plan every minute (Wooden 2005).

Wooden goes on to describe how every minute of every practice is carefully planned out ahead of time. After each practice, he jotted notes about what went well and what could have been improved. He filled reams of notebooks with these notes that went back for years and years. Each new year, he would review the previous year's schedule—day by day—and then create a new minute-by-minute plan.

Demonstrating that coaches' obsession with time isn't limited to the sport of basketball, former NFL coach of the New York Giants Tom Coughlin also dedicates a chapter to scheduling in his book *Earn the Right to Win*. Like other great leaders I've studied, Coughlin is obsessed literally with minutes. Of his typical schedule:

> For me the day usually begins at 5:20 A.M. with a workout, I'll be at my desk at 6:15 and will go until after 10:00

P.M. meetings. Every minute during the week is scheduled (Coughlin 2014).

Did I say he was obsessed with minutes? Actually, its seconds:

> Since it's impossible to create any more hours, I'll try to get more done in the time available by squeezing waste out of my schedule. I don't like to waste a second. Literally, a second.

In the more mundane competitive area of business, apparently a focus on minutes has been lost. A research project conducted by McKinsey revealed that about half of executives are not spending their time in a way that aligns with strategic priorities and one-third was "actively dissatisfied" with how they spend their time (Bevins and De Smet 2013).

What can they do about it?

THROW OUT YOUR TO-DO LIST

Could everything you know about time management be wrong? As research for my book *15 Secrets Successful People Know About Time Management*, I interviewed 7 billionaires, 13 Olympic athletes, 29 straight-A students, and 239 entrepreneurs. One of the findings shocked me: almost none of them used a to-do list.

How could this be? We've all been taught from the "Getting Things Done (GTD)" system and others that we put all our tasks onto a big list and then we prioritize that list. A1, A2, A3, B1, B2, C1 . . . Start working on A1, and when we're done, move on to A2.

It turns out to-do lists have many flaws. Research indicates that 41 percent of what we put on to-do lists are never done at all! And of the items that are done, many are jotted down and then crossed off the very same day (Adams 2014). Ahh, that felt good. How long have you had that unpleasant doctor visit on your list? Or maybe it's Christmas shopping, or cleaning out the garage. How many items have been sitting on your list for a month or longer?

To-do lists can also contribute to stress triggered by the Zeigarnik effect. This is the psychological term describing how, consciously or unconsciously, undone items flood our minds with uncontrolled thoughts. We just worked a ten-hour day but when we go home, rather than feeling productive and satisfied, our brain ruminates on all the things that are still on our list. Physically exhausted, we may toss and turn from insomnia, our brains still racing with the tasks we must tackle in the days ahead.

If you're not supposed to use a to-do list, what are you supposed to use?

Your calendar.

See, we've been lied to. GTD and most other time-management systems teach that while a to-do list is the place to manage your tasks, the calendar is used only for phone calls, meetings, and events (i.e., things that have specific start times).

Great leaders actually schedule everything. Instead of placing tasks on a to-do list, they pick a date, time, and duration and schedule it on their calendar. This is the only guaranteed way to know that you are investing your minutes in alignment with your values and goals. Known as time-blocking, when applied to everything, it can dramatically improve your—and your team's—results.

By way of example, my own calendar reflects many of my values:

- I value coaching my team members, so I time-block one-on-one meetings with each direct report on Mondays as a way to kick off the week.
- I value team alignment and breaking down silos, so I time-block a Weekly Action Review (WAR) meeting each week.
- I value writing so I have two to three blocks of time scheduled each week to write uninterrupted.
- I value health, so I time-block sixty minutes each day for exercise.
- I value my children's education, so I time-block evenings after dinner to help them with their homework.
- I value recharging and new experiences, so I block off long weekends or entire weeks—sometimes a year in advance—for vacations, even if I don't know yet where I'm going.

But what about free time? What about time to manage by walking around, or to just read, or to think strategically? Yes, you should schedule that, too. The CEO of LinkedIn, Jeff Weiner, in an article titled "The Importance of Scheduling Nothing," wrote:

> If you were to see my calendar, you'd probably notice a host of time slots greyed out but with no indication of what's going on. There is no problem with my Outlook or printer. The grey sections reflect "buffers," or time periods I've purposely kept clear of meetings.
>
> In aggregate, I schedule between 90 minutes and two hours of these buffers every day (broken down into 30- to 90-minute blocks). It's a system I developed over the last

several years in response to a schedule that was becoming so jammed with back-to-back meetings that I had little time left to process what was going on around me or just think (Weiner 2013).

If this is sounding crazy, remember that Hall of Fame sports coaches schedule their days by the minute, often planning an entire year in advance!

MATCH YOUR SCHEDULE TO YOUR ENERGY STATES

Military professionals use the term "force multiplier" to refer to the variables in battle that increase the effectiveness of a given number of troops. One hundred soldiers dug into defensive positions may be three times more effective than one hundred soldiers who are charging them offensively through an open field. Night-vision goggles are a force multiplier for those who have them. Reflecting on attitude and morale, General Colin Powell once said that perpetual optimism is a force multiplier.

Once you stop using a to-do list and begin to live each day from your calendar, not only will you begin to get more of the right things done and experience less stress, but you can leverage productivity multipliers by how you schedule your day. The real secret to time management is that it has nothing to do with time. What it's really about is energy and focused attention. We all have the same 1,440 minutes in a day.

Think about it. Let's say you have one hour to write a report. If you are totally alert, focused, and in the zone, how many words would you write in that hour? A thousand? Two thousand? But now imagine the same amount of time, sixty minutes, but this time you have flulike symptoms, or maybe you're hungover. Now how many words do you think you'll crank out? A few hundred? It's the same block of time, but your output, your productivity, will be vastly different.

For most people, we are cognitively at our best in the morning, generally about an hour or two after we first wake up. But the window stays open only for a brief time; we have about two hours until our creativity, focus, and decision making begin to decline. As behavioral psychologist Dan Ariely once answered in an online Reddit AMA (Ask Me Anything):

> One of the saddest mistakes in time management is the propensity of people to spend the two most productive hours of their day on things that don't require high cognitive capacity (like social media). If we could salvage those precious hours, most of us would be much more successful in accomplishing what we truly want (Ariely 2014).

If you reflect on your personal peak state times, you can factor this in as you schedule your week. Most of the high achievers I've interviewed over the years are fanatical about having a daily most important task, or MIT. The key is that they schedule time to work on it every single day, and it's usually in the morning (uninterrupted) before the rest of the day's events push it off.

My personal system for force multiplying my day is called the 3Cs: Create, Collaborate, Connect. On most days I:

- Create in the morning—do my writing, brainstorming, analysis, from about 7:00 a.m. to noon when I'm cognitively at my best

- Collaborate in the afternoon—hold all work-related meetings and phone calls from about 1:00 p.m. to 6:00 p.m.; interacting with others is less brain taxing and a bit energizing
- Connect in the evening—socially bond with family and friends from 7:00 p.m. to later in the evening, strengthening relationships while relaxing and recharging

Others talk about having just two categories: maker time and management time. But even this simple distinction helps you to pause and think through what a task is related to, and whether you should try to slot it into your peak energy time.

Last, when you move everything onto your calendar and are forced to assign a time duration, you will be less likely to default everything into half-hour or hour time slots. How often do you automatically just block off an entire hour when someone asks to "grab a coffee and catchup" or "pick your brain"? Remember the coaches' obsession: it's with minutes. What I heard repeatedly in my interviews was the more successful someone is, the smaller the amount of time their default is.

Jordan Harbinger, the host of *The Jordan Harbinger Show*, told me once, "Use a calendar and schedule your entire day into 15-minute blocks. It sounds like a pain, but this will set you up in the 95th percentile as far as organization goes. Use this not just for appointments, but workouts, calls, email blocks, etc." (Kruse 2015).

And bestselling author and cofounder of Likeable Media, Dave Kerpen, said, "If it's not in my calendar, it won't get done. But if it is in my calendar, it will get done. I schedule out every 15 minutes of every day to conduct meetings, review materials, write, and do any activities I need to get done" (Kruse 2015).

THE #1 THREAT TO YOUR TIME
(OR MARK CUBAN'S ADVICE)

I asked Mark Cuban a simple open-ended question: What is your number one piece of advice for productivity and time management?

What would the self-made billionaire who owns an NBA basketball team, stars on the hit TV show *Shark Tank*, owns dozens of other businesses, comments regularly on politics, and appears to be happily married with three kids tell me? Would he describe a unique way to prioritize a to-do list? Would he urge delegation? Perhaps he'd tell me to plan my day the night before? He answered with typical brevity and wit:

> Never take a meeting unless someone is writing you a check (Kruse 2015).

OF COURSE not all of us are in the position to refuse all meetings. But don't let Cuban's billionaire position blind you to the larger point. Of all the things he could have said, he focused on the dangers of meetings. In fact, I asked seven self-made billionaires the same question and most of them had some kind of advice about the dangers of meetings.

I'm sure this doesn't surprise you. In my survey research of over four thousand working professionals, meetings and emails tied as the number one productivity killer at work. Atlassian, a productivity software company, recently published data drawn from a series of studies conducted at Microsoft, the University of California, and other research centers (Atlassian n.d.). Here are a few of the biggest eye-openers:

- Most employees conduct at least sixty-two meetings a month.
- Half those meetings were considered a waste of time.
- An average of thirty-one hours per month were spent in unproductive meetings.

Great leaders know to minimize meetings at all costs not just for their own productivity, but for the productivity of their team, and to save the very real compensation costs to the organization. If you do an internet search for "meeting cost calculators," you'll find many online tools that will estimate the true cost of meetings by factoring in number of people, meeting duration, and salaries, and some will even mark up the salaries to cover benefits. Playing around with these calculators is interesting and horrifying at the same time.

For example, I use to run a weekly staff meeting of all my project managers to review project status and financial metrics. I had ten people in the meeting, it lasted for an hour, and the average salary of my project managers was about $80,000 plus 40 percent for benefits. This means that one meeting cost me $538.46. Was it worth it? Maybe, as it was a pretty important meeting that kept us all on track. Annualized I was spending $25,846 on these meetings. Really?! Hmm, now it makes me wonder if there was a way to share that information in a shared spreadsheet, or to do the meeting in thirty minutes instead.

THE SOLUTION TO THE MEETING PROBLEM

Great leaders know that every minute counts, and they know that meetings can potentially be a time killer. Meetings tend to start late, run long, they have the wrong people in them, they're dominated by the extroverts and showboaters, they stray off topic, and worst of all they break up your day in illogical ways. So what do you do about it?

First, if you're running the meeting, design it and facilitate it well. Make sure you have a well-planned agenda that clearly states the purpose of the meeting, desired outcomes, and initial topics. Circulate the agenda ahead of time so attendees arrive prepared. Think carefully about who to invite. The smaller the meeting, the more efficient it will be. Meetings must be actively facilitated: call on the introverts to weigh in with their opinions, silence side conversations, keep the conversation on topic, and manage the clock.

Second, even if you can't say no as often as Mark Cuban, perhaps you can say no to more meetings. Instead of automatically agreeing to every meeting invite that comes your way, ask for an agenda or for the desired outcome before accepting. At least this will train others to plan for a productive session. Or say no without saying no in these clever ways:

- "My schedule is really tight right now; how about I send Walter to represent me and he'll brief me afterward?"
- "Not sure I can make that; any chance you can send me the meeting minutes instead?"
- "That day is impossible; is it okay for me to only stay for the first twenty minutes?"

Or perhaps you can say no to meetings on certain days of the week. Sound crazy? Many organizations are beginning to implement "maker days." As Facebook cofounder and Asana CEO Dustin Moskovitz told me, "Pick one day a week that you and your team can focus on individual work without any interruptions like meetings . . . we have 'No Meeting Wednesdays' established to encourage flow and productivity across the company" (Kruse 2015). When my friend and hospital executive Kate Kinslow became CEO of Aria Healthcare, one of her first acts was to declare "No Meeting Fridays."

I mentioned this meeting-free-day idea to Rory Vaden, co-founder of Southwestern Consulting, and he laughed out loud. "We only have meetings one day a week," he exclaimed. "We call it Mad Meeting Mondays!" As the author of *Take the Stairs* and *Procrastinate on Purpose*, Vaden knows a thing or two about productivity. So I invited him onto *The LEADx Leadership Show* as my guest and he explained further.

> We've decided that the next generation business is one where people will work flexible hours, from multiple locations, on a variety of projects. Mondays are the one day we ask everyone to come in. We meet. We talk. We discuss. We make decisions. Then the rest of the week we scatter all across the world, we deploy those decisions, and we execute the strategies (Vaden 2017).

Southwestern Consulting's "four days off from meetings" culture may be extreme for most organizations, but it suddenly makes taking one day off from meetings each week seem much more realistic.

WHEN YOU JUST CAN'T SAY NO

For all those meetings that you just can't say no to, how can you keep their duration to a minimum? How can you maximize your time?

One idea is to hold "stand up" meetings, literally meetings where everyone stands up. This has become popular among leaders who practice Scrum, which is a project management framework for software development. A "daily scrum" is a stand-up meeting, usually about fifteen minutes in length, in which people go around and answer three questions:

1. What did you accomplish since the last meeting?
2. What do you plan to complete by the next meeting?
3. What is getting in your way?

Even though this format is most popular in software development, there is no reason why you can't adopt it for any kind of recurring status meeting.

Richard Branson has spoken extensively about his aversion to meetings. In one blog post, he shared that he uses the same trick for drastically shortening meeting time:

> One of my favourite tricks is to conduct most of my meetings standing up. I find it to be a much quicker way of getting down to business, making a decision and sealing the deal . . . it's very rare that a meeting on a single topic should need to last more than 5–10 minutes. If you stand up, you'll find that decisions get made pretty quickly, and no one nods off! (Branson 2015).

A variation of the stand-up meeting is the walking meeting, sometimes called the "walk and talk" with notable practitioners like Barack Obama, Mark Zuckerberg, Western Union CEO Hikmet Ersek, and Darren Huston, former president and CEO of Priceline (Talev and Hymowitz 2014). At LinkedIn, their outdoor bike path takes about twenty to twenty-five minutes to circle once and is routinely used by employees who are doing one-on-one meetings (Peck 2015). Meeting on the move removes the normal distractions from phones, email, and "got a minute" interruptions. Research from Johnson & Johnson shows that people who do walking meetings report higher levels of energy, focus, and engagement. And if you need more convincing, researchers at Stanford conducted experiments that revealed that walking boosts creative ideation (Oppezzo and Schwartz 2014).

HOW ONE CEO INSTANTLY INCREASED PRODUCTIVITY

"Wait, what?" I wasn't sure I heard him correctly.

"It's true," Hiren Doshi told me. "Your article was a pivotal point for me. I freed up six hours a day . . . over thirty hours per week."

Doshi is the cofounder and president of OmniActive Health Technologies, a leading supplier of nutritional ingredients with offices in India and the United States. For someone at his level of experience and success to make such a leap in productivity was shocking. The key, of course, was Doshi's epiphany around meetings.

> Six months ago I used to have crazy days, where I would do six to eight hours of meetings in a day, and also at night. But I brought it down to two hours a day of meetings, max. I suddenly realized that it was my need to be present; it was not my employees' need to have me there. So I told them I'm going to take a step back out of all these activities. Don't consider it disinterest from my side. Consider it my confidence in you. Everybody can step up and do a fine

job. Very often they do better than I did, and very often they didn't do as good a job as me. But guess what? The work got done and I scaled myself (Doshi 2017).

Doshi went on to say that he believes CEOs and other leaders are the ones calling for unnecessary meetings with their employees, partly because they have the wrong perception of their own importance. If you hired the right people, why do they need you in all their meetings (or sales calls, or presentations)?

So what did Doshi do when he suddenly had six free hours each day? "Creative thinking without interruption," he explained. With his time to think, and time to focus on new opportunities, Doshi began to execute on an acquisition strategy that could lead to exponential growth for the company. In fact, just months after I interviewed Doshi, OmniActive acquired the botanical extracts company Indfrag, in a deal worth $35 million.

THE TAKEAWAY

Great leaders understand the true value of time. You can never get a minute back once it's wasted. Whether you're a sports coach getting ready for the season, or an entrepreneur trying to ship your new product, or a manager who has to meet a deadline, using time more effectively is how you beat the competition. While traditional time-management systems teach us that our calendar is for meetings and phone calls, those who achieve extreme productivity put everything on their calendar and then live by that calendar.

HOW MIGHT YOU APPLY THIS IF YOU'RE A:

MANAGER: Becoming a "schedule don't list" kind of leader doesn't happen overnight. Begin by time-blocking everything that is important that tends to get blocked out by the urgent. Create recurring appointments with yourself to work on your most important task, schedule your team huddles and weekly one-on-ones, seize blocks of time only to "THINK!"

SALES PROFESSIONAL: Salespeople have to juggle prospecting and selling to new clients with servicing existing clients and tackling all that administrative work. For many that means clients come first, paperwork is submitted late, and prospecting doesn't happen at all. Consider time-blocking Friday afternoons for admin time, and the first hour of each day for prospecting.

SPORTS COACH: Whether you are a volunteer youth coach also managing your "real" job or you're facing endless demands as a professional coach, you are acutely aware that there is never enough time. Take a page from the playbook of Coach K, Wooden, and Coughlin and plan your team practices in advance and run them with a stopwatch. Carefully consider your priorities and schedule them onto your daily calendar. Your smartphone calendar suddenly becomes your "to do" list.

MILITARY OFFICER: When you're deployed, work-life balance isn't an issue, because there is no hope for balance. But even back home the time demands on military personnel are extraordinary. There is no getting around the fact that the day has only so many hours, which must be divided between your leadership duties, your family, and your own personal health and welfare. Get clear on your personal values and translate those values into an allocation of your time, and then map those hours onto your calendar. Remember, schedule don't list.

PARENT: They say you can tell what someone truly values by how they spend their time. I know you love your kids more than anything—you probably value them above all else. But do you spend more time with them, or dusting the house? Do you stay late in the office only when times truly demand it, or most of the time? Consider scheduling a stop working time; put on your calendar "Go home now." As former Intel CEO Andy Grove said, "There will always be more to do, and more than can be done." If you live from your to-do list, there will always be more to do. Live from your calendar, time-block family dinners or homework or reading at bedtime, and ensure that your time matches your values.

INDIVIDUAL: Leadership begins by leading yourself first. Too often we let others lead us . . . lead us to responding to their crises, solving their problems, putting out their fires. But remember, if you aren't working on your goals, you're working on someone else's goals. What do you truly value? What are your goals in each of these areas? Now time-block daily or weekly chunks of time to pursue these life goals. Whether it's a daily workout in the gym, or a weekly review of your financials, or a monthly day away with your spouse, protect that time at all costs.

7

I was leading a team of about 250 people and one of my direct reports, Shawn, let me know that he had a tough conversation with one of his direct reports.

"She had a long list of grievances but basically she accused me of playing favorites," he began.

Shawn was one of my best team members and totally committed to the company. He was in the office working by six or seven in the morning and was still there when most people were heading home at night. He was also known for having a bit of a temper and for joking and teasing team members. I immediately cringed, thinking this was going to turn into an HR headache that I just didn't have the time or stomach for.

"So what did you say?" I was hoping he had a good defense.

"I told her she was right," he said with a chuckle. "I do play favorites."

"What?"

Up until that time I had a simplistic view of fairness. Managers shouldn't be biased or attached to some team members more than others; they should treat everyone on their teams the same. In fact, I probably thought it was unethical to play favorites.

Shawn, in what could be seen as a case of "mentoring up," proceeded to explain his leadership style.

"I told her I do play favorites. I spend more time with my high performers than my low performers. I give more opportunities to those who show potential. I even handle mistakes differently for those who rarely make them than those who make them all the time."

This idea intrigued me, and I was still worried about his upset employee. I asked, "So what was her response to that?"

"She said, 'OK, so tell me what I need to do to become a favorite.'"

FAVORITISM ISN'T CRONYISM

Many managers were like I was before Shawn showed me the light. Without really thinking it through, we take at face value the idea that treating everyone the same is what's fair. Treating people equally seems fair or even ethical. Here in the US perhaps it's our deep-rooted attachment to the view that, "all men are created equal." Perhaps it's a stretch of our moral foundation in which we would never want to treat anyone differently based on their gender, age, race, religion, or sexual orientation. And let me be clear, playing favorites based on any of that would be wrong! Favoritism doesn't mean discrimination.

It could also be that we confuse favoritism with cronyism, the practice of giving preferential treatment or jobs based on friendship or some special affiliation and not because of merit. Favoritism doesn't mean changing the rules or performance standards. The rules apply to everybody; it's just that the consequences are different.

Of course, while all people might be created equal, by the time they're employees on your team they have very different:

- Talents
- Experiences
- Attitudes
- Skills
- Communication styles
- Learning styles
- Career goals
- Needs
- Engagement

People are different, so treating everyone the same doesn't mean we're treating them fairly. In fact, that would be very unfair.

I wish I had understood this earlier in my career. It would have saved me from a lot of stress and time-consuming conversations:

- No, we can't buy a $1,000 ergonomic chair for Sam even though his doctor says he has a bad back because then we'll have to buy a $1,000 chair for everyone.
- No, we can't let Andrea leave work at 4:00 every day just because she has bad night vision, because then we'll have to let everyone go home at 4:00.

- No, we can't let two junior people move into the offices with windows even though they are empty right now, because the rule is only director-level people get offices.

It wasn't just individual requests that I didn't know how to deal with, it was issues related to the standards and culture of an entire company. I remember one of my team leaders, Karla, who was having a great year bringing in revenue and profits at a much higher level than the other teams. She was literally making me millions of dollars. Karla was charismatic, and slowly her team began to form its own identity. They created their own mission statement and values to supplement the ones we already had. I would hold town hall meetings and quarterly retreats, and Karla began to do her own team-level events right after mine. It didn't take long for several people to come to me to ask why Karla's team was allowed to have their own subculture. Why are they special? Doesn't it go against the spirit of "one team"? It's not fair!

Because I didn't understand that it's okay to treat people differently, I struggled with the issue myself. I probably mumbled something like, "As long as what she is doing doesn't outright conflict with our values and culture I'm okay with it." But basically I let the issue linger forever. Karla knew people were grumbling about her and it didn't seem like I had her back. The grumblers themselves felt slighted because I was playing favorites and it seemed unfair.

What I later learned, and what you'll read below, is, yes, teamwork is important. But sometimes when you have a star player—someone who is outperforming the others by a lot— they *deserve* to be treated differently.

FIRM BUT FLEXIBLE; LATITUDE TO LEAD

In 1992, *Chicago Tribune* writer Sam Smith wrote a tell-all book about the Chicago Bull's 1990–1991 championship season in the NBA. The book was called *The Jordan Rules*, which was originally a reference to a rival team's strategy for dealing with the greatest basketball player of all time, Michael Jordan (Smith 1993). But it took on a second meaning as Jordan was treated differently by the Bulls' coaches, team owners, and even referees. While *Jordan's Rules* caused a bit of a stir when it was released, the fact that star athletes are treated differently would surprise no one who has ever coached at any level.

The greatest basketball coach of all time, John Wooden, described how he evolved on this very issue in his book *Wooden on Leadership* (Wooden 2005). When he first started coaching, he would tell his players that he would treat them all the same because that was what was fair, and he was trying to be impartial. He goes on to write:

> Gradually I began to suspect that it was neither fair nor impartial. In fact, it was just the opposite. That's when I began announcing that team members wouldn't be treated the same or alike; rather, each one would receive the treatment they earned and deserved. This practice may sound discriminatory or suggest partiality, but it is neither.

Mike "Coach K" Krzyzewski, in his book *Leading with the Heart,* suggests that many leaders like setting rules because it's easier (Krzyzewski 2001). They don't actually have to think about the best way to handle each situation. While more difficult, he learned that the best thing to do was to stay flexible. He wrote:

Take being late for practice as an example. If a senior like Tommy Amaker, who's done everything right for nearly four years, is suddenly late for a team bus or a team meeting, I would wait a couple of minutes for him. He's built up trust by being on time over the long haul . . . However with a new player who has yet to build trust, I might be less flexible.

Coach K calls his preference for flexibility the "latitude to lead." It's important to note that the rules stay the same for everyone; it's the punishment that changes. It wouldn't be fair to insist some players have to show up for meetings on time and others don't. But it is fair to take into consideration the larger context of the situation when determining how to handle it.

NFL Super Bowl champion Gary Brackett played for the Indianapolis Colts for nine years. After retiring from American football, he went back to school to earn his MBA and today owns and manages Stacked Pickle, a restaurant franchise with ten locations. When he came on *The LEADx Leadership Show* I asked him for his number one piece of advice for new managers. His answer interestingly was almost exactly what Coach K said.

My management style is that you don't treat everyone equal, you treat everyone fair. The people that are inside your four walls who have been on time for the last three years, but for one week when she's dealing with her car problems she's been late, versus the guy who's been on for three months and he's been late every week since the day he started. They're not the same individual. Understanding both of those scenarios, I treat them very differently inside our restaurant. It's what really buys loyalty and buy-in from our staff (Brackett 2017).

The best coaches don't play favorites based on who they like better; rather, they give preferential treatment based on those who've earned it.

PLAYING FAVORITES WITH YOUR TIME

Cy Wakeman is a successful entrepreneur who now studies and consults on workplace drama. In her book *Reality-Based Leadership*, she encourages us to "work with the willing" first (Wakeman 2010). These are the best people on your team who show up each day fully engaged, who proactively offer their ideas and solutions, and who are most productive. Wakeman estimates that about 20 percent of workers fall into this category, and our challenge is to keep them (i.e., to retain them), as this is the group that will always have the most career options available to them.

Wakeman also describes the mirror image of this group, the other 20 percent who seem to always complain, resist change, or cause trouble. Yet this is the group that most of us, as managers, spend our time on. We spend extra time giving them constructive feedback, coaching, and mentoring. We spend extra time listening to their complaints. We spend extra time on discipline. Wakeman's own research suggests that one problem employee results in an extra eighty hours a year of work for the manager.

I look back at my own leadership trajectory and cringe at how hard I worked trying to get these people to be happy. Linda claimed to have low blood pressure that caused her to feel cold all the time. She would walk through my open door each week with a new request. Can you raise the temperature on the thermostat? Can I move my desk away from the window? Can you call the HVAC company to change the vent above my desk?

Can I move my desk away from the vent? Can you buy me a space heater? Can you take away the space heater because now it's too hot? Can I work from home where it isn't so cold? The crazy thing was that I actually tried to accommodate all these endless requests. Today I'm more likely to say, "Linda, do you own a sweater?"

In fact, I've come to take a very hard line when it comes to those who fall into the category that Gallup labels "actively disengaged." According to their most recent "State of the American Workplace" study, 16 percent of employees fall into this category of people who are "miserable in the workplace and destroy what the most engaged employees build" (Gallup 2017). As I speak at conferences and company retreats all around the world I'm frequently asked about what to do with this group. Individual managers will ask, "My overall engagement scores are really high and almost everyone on the team is fully engaged, but there is one woman who I just can't seem to get to. How do I engage that last person on my team?"

My answer always surprises people: Just fire her. You can do it kindly, you can do it with compassion, you can help her find a new job elsewhere, but you should force her not to work on your team. Let me be clear, I'm not talking about the vast number of average performers who are "not engaged" (i.e., neither actively engaged, nor actively disengaged). I'm talking about the small number of people who are chronically negative. These are the people who, when asked on surveys, say they are dissatisfied in their job, they wouldn't refer friends to the company, and they frequently think of working elsewhere. As Wakeman points out repeatedly in her book, we can't change people. These actively disengaged people are probably hiring mistakes. Maybe they're a lawyer because their parents told them to be, but they hate being a lawyer. Maybe they enjoy working in IT, but they prefer a sandals-and-T-shirt Silicon Valley culture over your khaki-and-button-down New York City culture. Maybe they are feeling angry after their two-hour one-way commute each morning. Whatever their issue is, it's their issue, not yours.

The danger of investing a disproportionate amount of time with our problem employees is the cost of not spending that time and attention with the other team members. This is time that we could spend "re-recruiting" our stars to make sure they don't get lured away by another company. This is time we could spend coaching our middle group of workers, moving some of them from average to stars. Think about your own team members, and think about whom you spent time with over the last week. Are you investing your effort in the right people?

ENGAGE PEOPLE THE SAME, BUT DIFFERENTLY

Are people around the world all motivated the same way? Actually, yes they are, but . . .

In my book *We: How to Increase Performance and Profits Through Full Engagement*, my coauthor Rudy Karsan and I share the analysis of survey results from ten million workers in 150 countries (Karsan and Kruse 2011). We identified a dozen drivers of "engagement"—the emotional connection one has to their employer and its goals—and zeroed in on three primary drivers: growth, recognition, and trust. People want to learn, grow, and advance in their careers. People want to feel appreciated by their managers and peers. People want to trust senior leadership, but not just from an ethics standpoint; they want to "trust" that leadership has a plan for the future and will successfully guide the organization to its goals.

As I lectured managers around the world to focus on growth, recognition, and trust, I would often be asked about cultural differences. "How can you say that everyone around the world is motivated the same way?" The secret is that on a macro level the drivers apply to everyone, but on a micro level you individualize how to apply it.

After all, it would be rare to find someone who says, "No, I don't want to grow and advance in my career. Next year I want to be dumber and paid less." But as a leader how you would activate the growth driver in a twenty-five-year-old might be different from how you would activate it for a sixty-year-old who is only a few years away from retirement. For the less experienced employee you might hold frequent career-path conversations, send her to training seminars, and offer graduate school tuition reimbursement. For the more senior employee you might enlist him to be a mentor or trainer to the younger workers, and he'd have to learn new skills as a teacher.

Similarly, it would be hard to find someone—anywhere in the world—who would say, "I just worked a hundred hours last week and totally blew past my goals. But I'd rather my boss not notice and just treat me like all the other slackers around here." Most people hope that they are appreciated. But once again, how you show appreciation will vary person to person. I concede that there are cultural norms around the world. Workplace birthday celebrations that might include balloons, cakes, and singing in America are, I'm told, far more restrained in the Netherlands. Despite HR nervousness, I've seen plenty of high fives and hugs among colleagues here in America, while in China . . . you don't see that too much.

The main takeaway is to treat each person as an individual; engage each person individually. Not in accordance to gender norms, or cultural norms, and certainly not "the same." Tune in to how your team members prefer to be recognized. Maybe Ian beams with pride when he gets a big shout-out in the weekly team meeting. Maybe that would embarrass Christine and she'd prefer a handwritten thank-you note instead. How do they like to grow and develop? Maybe Bella learns best by reading books, while Gianna likes to learn in workshops. How will they best see how their work is aligned to the bigger organizational goals? Abby maybe only needs to hear the message from the CEO once to remember it. Ellie might need the company's annual goals printed out and pinned on her cubicle wall. It's certainly easier to treat everyone the same, but it's not effective. Take the time to discover how to activate each team member's engagement triggers.

CATS, DOGS, AND GOLDEN BUDDHAS

"If I were hiring for someone to fetch sticks out of the pond in front of the house, and a cat applies for the job and it has a master's degree in stick-fetching . . ." This was how Dave Munson began when I asked him to give advice to new managers who might be listening to *The LEADx Leadership Show* (Munson 2017). Munson is one of the most entertaining and larger-than-life people I've ever interviewed. As the founder and CEO of Saddleback Leather, he's grown it from selling a single bag a month to a 15-million-dollar-a-year business. And there have been a lot of twists and turns in his journey. As he says on his website, "A hot wife, two fabulous kids, 14 Rwandan sons and daughters, a cool dog and a crooked federale sent to kill me kind of makes up the Saddleback story." And he left out his bullfighting and the three years he lived in a $100-a-month apartment without hot water in Juarez, Mexico. But back to his advice . . .

". . . and then a Lab shows up, and he's all wet, I would totally hire the Lab! I wouldn't ask the cat to go swimming all day long fetching sticks." Munson is talking about hiring the right person for the right job. And the right person isn't necessarily the one with the right education or résumé, it's the person who has a natural trait—or strength—for the kind of job you have in mind. To me, the key piece of Munson's advice is when he mentioned that the Lab showed up already wet. As one of my mentors, Bill Erickson, once told me, a true strength isn't just something you're good at or that you like to do. A true strength is something you can't not do.

With this definition in mind I think of my buddy Ian who is one of the most gifted sales professionals I've ever met. He's a true relator. Now, I've had some sales success in my own life, too, but I had to force myself to do it. It was painful! As a massive introvert, I hate going out on sales calls, I hate cold-calling, in fact, I even hate calling people I already know! But Ian is different. I think he feels best when he's on the phone talking to someone. He likes talking to fifty people a day. He gets energized by it. In fact, the way I feel when I'm cold-calling someone is probably how he feels sitting at home on the couch with nothing but a book in his hand.

While average leaders might try to assign work in some standard way to be fair, great leaders give different jobs to different people based on innate talents and highly developed skills. And beyond that, they let different people do the same job in different ways. I learn about different team members' strengths by watching what they do well, what they do poorly, and by asking a lot of questions:

- If you could be doing any job at all, what would it be?
- When was the last time you felt you were in the zone— you know, when you lost all track of time—what were you doing?

- What would you like to be doing five years from now?
- What do you hate doing? What tasks are superboring?

I think one of the biggest gifts leaders can give others is to identify or encourage the development of a gift that someone doesn't even know she has. When it comes to uncovering our strengths, or gifts, I can't help but think of the statue known as the Golden Buddha. In 1955, in Bangkok, Thailand, a ten-foot-tall clay statue of the Buddha was being moved to a new location. In the process, a piece broke off to reveal that it was actually a pure gold statue that had only been covered in clay. With today's price of gold the statue is worth $250 million dollars, but its true value had been hidden for over six hundred years. After much research, historians concluded that the Golden Buddha was likely covered in twelve inches of clay by Buddhist monks to hide it from Burmese invaders. When the monks were killed by their attackers, the knowledge of what lay beneath the clay died with them.

We are born with and develop certain strengths, but often they get covered up by our own limiting beliefs; we lack the confidence to pursue our true calling. I've actually encouraged several people in the past to switch their job function to go into sales. While they were all initially skeptical, those who have made the move quickly moved into six-figure careers and within years were happily earning exponentially more than they were before. One of the greatest gifts you can give your team members is to be the light that shines on their natural strengths.

WHICH OF YOUR CHILDREN IS YOUR FAVORITE?

A couple of weeks ago I heard a strange whirring sound in my home. I raced to the living room and to my utter bafflement and delight, I saw my daughter Amanda vacuuming the rug. My other daughter, Natalie, was lying on the couch doing nothing. Once I overcame the shock of the unasked-for housecleaning I naturally whipped out my phone, activated Snapchat, and recorded a video of my vacuuming daughter while I sang loudly "My favorite daughter, my favorite daughter!" And then I immediately panned to Natalie on the couch and sang "Not my favorite daughter, not my favorite daughter!"

Oh, the Dad humor! The reality is that I'm so nervous about scarring my kids with perceived favoritism that when the first draft of this book is done, I'll count up the number of times I mention Amanda, Natalie, and Owen and I'll add and delete stories until they've each been mentioned the same number of times.

Research from UC Davis professor Katherine Conger indicates I have reason to be on guard. She found that 70 percent of fathers and 74 percent of mothers admitted to researchers that they show favoritism toward one of their children (Shebloski, Conger, and Widaman 2005).

Studies vary but predictors of favoritism include birth order, gender, and personality. And indeed, offering varying degrees of love, attention, or material goods based on this is bad and leads to all kinds of negative family dynamics and increased dysfunction for the child who isn't favored.

But parents can show favoritism—officially called parental differential treatment—with their kids in ways similar to a manager playing favorites at work. Your standards for behavior should be different for toddlers than for teens. Punishment for missing curfew might be lighter for a child who has never been late before, versus one who is a habitual offender. You should encourage the natural interests and strengths of each child (rather than just being a soccer family, for example). Consistent favoritism for the wrong reasons can hurt a family, but parental differentiation for the right reasons sends strong signals as to what gets rewarded in the home and leads to the development of one's true strengths.

PLAYING FAVORITES IN THE MILITARY

"We salute, Marine." Colonel Chris Dowling gave a stern reminder to a young marine in the chow line. In what was one of the most memorable days of my life, I visited Marine Corps Recruit Depot (MCRD) San Diego on the day when boot camp recruits finished a grueling fifty-four-hour-long test called the Crucible. With little sleep or food over the previous two days, dozens of recruits had just earned the right to be called US Marines, and now having little sleep or food over the previous two days, they were in line for the cafeteria where the "Warriors Breakfast" awaited them. As we walked past the newly minted marines, most snapped a crisp salute to Colonel Dowling. But several did not. And each time, the colonel would stop and say, "We salute, Marine." And after he received the salute, we'd walk on down the line until it happened again.

When I asked him about it, he told me he was just giving them a reminder. He said normally, if it had been a week earlier and a recruit didn't salute him, he would have asked them to drop and do push-ups, or worse. While he wasn't going to ignore the infraction, he said he knew that the men were standing there half asleep and probably just didn't see him coming. These marines just off the Crucible were being reprimanded differently than other nonsaluting marines would have been. Same standard, not to be ignored, but with variable punishment.

Seeing how to match someone's strength to a job can sometimes literally be easy to see. Retired Marine Corps colonel John Boggs told me about a big young recruit he once had who was physically gifted but struggled with the simplest of rules. Rules as basic as putting "sir" at the beginning or end of each sentence. Colonel Boggs assigned the recruit to be his squad's designated automatic rifleman, which is the marine who carries the big machine gun. Now, with purpose and pride, the young M249 "gunner" became a consummate marine.

Usually it takes extra effort for a military leader to develop subordinate leaders in accordance with their strengths. In an article published in the *Military Review*, US Army psychologist Melinda Key-Roberts writes that it's a core tenet of army doctrine that nurturing strengths (not just correcting deficiencies) is the key to developing subordinate leaders to their full potential (Key-Roberts 2014). Unfortunately too many army leaders default to using the Army's Evaluation Reporting System (AERS) or Officer Evaluation Reports (OER) when it comes to identifying strengths. That's like a corporate manager using HR's annual performance review to consider strengths. Neither work well as forward-looking methods for leader development.

Among other things, Dr. Key-Roberts suggests that army leaders need to make the time to identify the strengths of subordinate leaders, to give individualized specific feedback, and to utilize talent even if it's outside one's identified specialty. As one officer told her:

I have one guy who's great—he's the PT stud. The other guy's a horrible PT guy . . . but [he's] good at commo. He's my commo NCO, and that's how I handle him. . . . He's not [actually] a commo NCO, he's a scout, but he's good at it [commo]—he knows what he's doing. . . . Seeing what he's good at [I say] "ok man, you're my communications NCO."

Another officer gave this example:

At the end of the day, I would assign the lieutenant who had great communication skills to be the guy who would interact at a more complex level with the Iraqi Security Forces, and the guy who was completely inarticulate but could kick down the door and do raids is the guy I would generally assign to more kinetic operations.

THE TAKEAWAY

In a misguided attempt to be objective and fair, too many managers treat all their team members the same. That's an extremely unfair way to treat your best performers, and they'll surely leave for better opportunities when they see they benefit no better than the slackers. When it comes to discipline, great leaders know that while the rules and standards need to apply to everyone—and treating everyone the same is easier than having to make decisions—the consequence of infractions should vary based on circumstances. Great leaders also know to take the time to identify each person's strengths and then align opportunities and career path options to take advantage of them.

HOW MIGHT YOU APPLY THIS IF YOU'RE A:

MANAGER: Take extra time to get to know your new team members. Ask them what they are doing when they are performing at their best. Ask them what they like doing when they're not at work. Consider purposely mixing up roles and assignments and see how people perform. When it comes to infractions, remember to use the same rules and standards, but vary the punishments.

SALES PROFESSIONAL: Great salespeople know that not all clients are equal. Do you spend as much time visiting your unprofitable clients as you do your profitable ones? Do you "wine and dine" your small accounts as often as your large? Consider plotting all your customers on a matrix. How valuable is each client versus how hard are they to service? The ones that are high value and low hassle are the ones you want to play favorites with.

SPORTS COACH: The next time a player breaks a rule—whether showing up late to a meeting or with a dress code infraction—consider the big picture. Do they have a pattern of disrespect or is it just an unusual mistake? Vary the punishment accordingly. Coach K is known for changing his practice methods and game strategy every year when he gets new players. Do your current players need to focus on the same drills that you used with last year's players? How should you best use your players in the game—are they more of a set offense team, or a fast break team?

MILITARY OFFICER: With all the mandatory requirements and time demands, military leaders need to remember that they are tasked with the development of subordinate leaders. Make it a priority to look beyond rank and Military Occupation Specialty (MOS) code to identify and further utilize someone's strengths. Watch and listen as you observe people work, ask people what they're good at, assign tasks that are outside their normal duties.

PARENT: It is more dangerous to be a parent who is unaware she has a favorite child than to be one who acknowledges it and adjusts. Be on the lookout for consistent favoring behaviors just because you like one child more than another (you can still love them all the same). Instead, remember that you can individualize expectations, punishments, and activities based on the ages and behaviors of your kids.

INDIVIDUAL: As an adult, playing favorites in the traditional sense of the word is healthy and to be encouraged. Think about all your family members and friends who you routinely interact with. Which ones make you feel happy and good about yourself? Which ones are unsupportive and seem to make you feel bad after you talk to them? You deserve to be happy and have the right to cut out negativity in your life—even if it means reducing the time you spend with certain family members. (Oh, the guilt!) How can you spend more time with your favorite friends? How can you give extra time, attention, and support to your favorite friends?

8

REVEAL EVERYTHING (EVEN SALARIES)

I magine that your manager, Ray, invited you and four of your colleagues to meet with him. After the hour-long meeting concludes, you walk out of the conference room frustrated and angry. What a waste of time! It's so rude to call for a meeting and not even be ready for it! When you get back to your desk, you decide to send your boss an email so he knows exactly what you think of him. You write:

Ray—you deserve a "D-" for your performance today in the meeting . . . you did not prepare at all because there is no way you could have, and been that disorganized. In the future, I would ask you to take some time and prepare and maybe even I should come up and start talking to you to get you warmed up or something but we can't let this happen again.

Would you ever send your boss an email like that?

Now imagine that your boss, Ray, is one of the hundred richest men in the world. He's the founder and CEO of the company. The company in fact is the world's largest hedge fund with $160 billion in assets. Would that make it harder or easier to send that email?

The email above is real. It was sent by an employee of Bridgewater Associates to his boss, Ray Dalio, one of the world's richest men and most successful investors. Rather than being offended, rather than punishing his employee for insubordination, Dalio gleefully shared this email in his TED talk titled, "How to Build a Company Where the Best Ideas Win" (Dalio 2017). At Bridgewater Associates, sharing everything isn't just limited to company information; it includes real-time feedback on all your colleagues' ideas and behaviors. Dalio explained that his experience of being overly confident and eventually wrong in the early 1980s—which cost him his business and all his personal wealth—drove him to build a culture that would foster better decision making.

> I wanted to find the smartest people who would disagree with me to try to understand their perspective or to have them stress test my perspective. I wanted to make an idea meritocracy. In other words, not an autocracy in which I would lead and others would follow and not a democracy in which everybody's points of view were equally valued, but I wanted to have an idea meritocracy in which the best ideas would win out. And in order to do that, I realized that we would need radical truthfulness and radical transparency . . . people needed to say what they really believed and to see everything.

And when he says "to see everything," he really means it. All meetings at Bridgewater are videotaped and every employee can watch the recordings, which are stored online in their "Transparency Library." Special manager meetings called "drilldowns" are held to diagnose problems and craft solutions. While the Bridgewater Associates culture is unusual, so are their results.

RADICAL TRANSPARENCY FERTILIZES GREAT CULTURE

There aren't many leaders who are as obsessed with idea meritocracy as Ray Dalio, and not everyone thrives in an environment of real-time group judgment. But the trend is clear: highly successful leaders are now operating in a model of radical transparency. They share everything.

This goes against centuries-long practices where people believed, "Information is power." Meaning those who had it had power over those who didn't. With the traditional view that business is a zero-sum game—we're both sales reps and only one of us will get promoted to sales manager this year—I'm incentivized not to help you, lest you improve your performance and beat me out. If you and I both run company business units and fight for annual budget allocations, cooperating with you just takes dollars out of my budget for next year. If we're fellow project managers, and you ask if I know any good freelance software engineers, my first thought would be that if you hire my favorite freelancer, she then won't be available to work on my projects.

Yet, in the new world of work, we win or lose based on the strength of the team, not the individual. What's the point of winning 5 percent more budget dollars or getting that promotion if we're going to be out of business in two years? As leaders in the twenty-first century we have to realize that radical transparency—sharing everything—is like a fertilizer for so many valuable things.

First, radical transparency provides the situational awareness your team members need to make good decisions quickly. There is no time for information seeking, information clearance, kicking decisions up the chain of command. We need real-time data so sales reps can answer prospects questions quickly, we need shared goals so employees can align their work, we need financial transparency so our workers spend wisely, and we need to even share our failures for collective learning and to foster a culture of risk-taking and innovation.

Second, radical transparency directly drives employee engagement. In my own experience as a business leader and based on my previous analysis of over ten million employee surveys, communication is one of the top four drivers of employee engagement. Employees want more information, all the time. It's impossible to overcommunicate. Transparent companies by default are in total communication mode as standard operating practice. While Ray Dalio takes this practice to the extreme, there is a good reminder from Bridgewater that transparency can and should flow in all directions. What do your team members think of you as a leader? Maybe sending an email isn't the right mechanism to find out, but transparent organizations will do things like 360-evaluations, employee surveys, and digital idea boxes to find out.

Third, radical transparency drives trust (which drives engagement). According to the 2017 Edelman Trust Barometer, there has been "an implosion of trust" as public trust in government officials, business leaders, and the media are at an all-time low (Edelman 2017). In fact, the percent of people who say they trust their CEO dropped 12 percentage points in one year, from 49 percent in 2016 to 37 percent in 2017. One way to lose trust is to actually lie and get caught. But a more common way is to only give good news. Too many leaders believe what Colonel Jessup (played by Jack Nicholson) believed in *A Few Good Men*: "You can't handle the truth!" When our leaders only share good news, good financial results, wins, strengths, and opportunities, we know we're only getting half the picture. It's a lie by omission.

We need our team members to be fully informed so they can make good decisions quickly, and we need them to be fully engaged so they'll give discretionary effort to the cause. Radical transparency is the driver for both.

FROM "KNOWLEDGE IS POWER" TO "SHARING IS POWER"

The military is not the place you'd expect to learn lessons about transparency and the distribution of sensitive information. The very idea of a hierarchical command-and-control structure emanated from the Roman army, and post-industrial-revolution companies were inspired by the military culture of following orders without question. So, too, in dealing with matters of life and death, information is often considered classified and available on a need-to-know basis.

Indeed, it was this culture of silos, information hoarding, and lack of trust that existed when US Army general Stanley McChrystal assumed command of the Joint Special Operations Command (JSOC) Task Force in 2003. His mission was to defeat al-Qaeda in Iraq, which was a self-organizing, rapidly adapting enemy unlike any he had faced before. In an interview after his retirement, McChrystal explained that the traditional system of information flowing up the organization and decisions flowing back down was no longer effective. He said:

> To defeat an enemy like Al Qaeda in Iraq (AQI), we had to beat them at their own game—the phrase it takes a network to defeat a network became our mantra. We created radical transparency through widespread information sharing and pushed decision-making down to the lowest levels (Pope 2015).

In his book *Team of Teams*, McChrystal goes into greater detail about his goal to achieve a "shared consciousness" among his own team and partnering organizations that would enable decision making at the lowest levels, which he calls empowered execution. He writes:

> Shared consciousness demanded the adoption of extreme transparency throughout our force and with our partner forces. This was not "transparency" in the sense that it is usually used in the business world, a synonym for personal candidness. We needed transparency that provided every team with an unobstructed, constantly up-to-date view of the rest of the organization (McChrystal 2015).

Over the course of five years, as General McChrystal slowly changed the culture, the fight against AIQ became more successful. In a TED talk, McChrystal summarized the secret to success: "We had to change our culture about information . . . instead of knowledge is power, to one where sharing is power" (McChrystal 2014).

This idea of providing as much information and decision-making authority as possible to frontline operators is echoed also in the work of US Marine Corps general Charles Krulak. In 1999, he wrote an article for *Marines Magazine* titled, "The Strategic Corporal: Leadership in the Three Block War" (Krulak 1999). The term "Three Block War" served as a metaphor for the simultaneous demands placed on frontline marines. On one block, they may be doing humanitarian work. One block away, they may be in peacekeeping mode. On the third block, marines are in actual combat. To be successful, decision-making power must rest in the field with the lowest level of noncommissioned officer, the corporal. He writes that an outcome:

> . . . may hinge on decisions made by small unit leaders, and by actions taken at the lowest level. The Corps is, by design, a relatively young force. Success or failure will rest, increasingly, with the rifleman and with his ability to make the right decision at the right time at the point of contact.

Krulak also points out that the decision made by a young marine on the other side of the world could be headline news the next day, and even have strategic impact. This truth is heightened by the ubiquity today of mobile phones with cameras and the ability to distribute instantly via social media. In order for frontline leaders to make the right decisions, they need to be clear on the strategic intent of senior leaders and they must have total situational awareness—the same information that their generals have.

OPEN-BOOK MANAGEMENT

Kris Boesch arrived at work as the new CEO of a moving company. With no prior experience in the industry, she found a workplace so toxic that employees were openly cursing at each other and ready to come to blows. Financially, the company was on the verge of collapse. Over time, with a focus on purpose, open-book management, and workplace culture her employees soon thrived and she was able to save the company.

Boesch wrote about her experience and lessons learned in her book, *Culture Works: How to Create Happiness in the Workplace* (Boesch 2017). When I interviewed her on *The LEADx Leadership Show* she shared how she began to teach her employees about the financials. She described how she gathered everyone and did an activity she called "Connect the mission to the money, and the money to the mission" (Boesch 2017).

> I'd get 100 one-dollar bills and I'd do it in percentages. I'd say, "Okay, you're my rent, you're my marketing, you're my insurance," and I would hand the money out. I would do payroll last and say, "This is what we have at the end of the day," and that's to pay debt, and if we want to buy new trucks."
>
> There was just this whole, "Oh, my gosh. That's where the money goes. No, she's not lining her basement with gold bricks." All of a sudden there was awareness of how we made our money and how we spent it.
>
> I would also tell them, "Listen, to want to grow and increase our revenue is not a greed factor. It comes from our

desire to expand our mission. The more money we have, the more people we can serve. The more people we serve, the more money we have."

My guys would come back and say, "Oh, my gosh. I can help with truck repairs, and I'm not going to forget a moving blanket because that's twelve bucks, and that's two hours of profit."

Just make sure you're always communicating the "why" behind the numbers and the money.

Open-book management is a practice in which every employee, from CEO to janitor, has access to all the organization's financial information and is trained in how to understand it. The idea is largely credited to Jack Stack, who bought an almost bankrupt engine remanufacturing company and turned it around by empowering employees with the financials. He later described his process in a book called *The Great Game of Business* (Stack 2013). Over the years, in books, speeches, and workshops, the system has been taught to thousands of companies. Many coaches of open-book systems claim the one-year financial increase is in the neighborhood of 30 percent. Stack has summarized the system as:

1. **Know and Teach the Rules.** Every employee should be given the measures of business success and taught how to understand them.
2. **Follow the Action and Keep Score.** Every employee should be expected and enabled to act on his or her knowledge to improve performance.
3. **Provide a Stake in the Outcome.** Every employee should have a direct stake in the company's success and risk of failure.

With my own businesses I credit open-book management as one of the keys behind just surviving as a company, to thriving with exponential growth. At first I wasn't doing it right. I was sharing all the financials, but it consisted of me handing out profit-and-loss statements and balance sheets and walking them through it. I'd ask if there were any questions, but no hands went up. It was hard for them to raise their hands when they were asleep with their eyes open.

What I learned was to basically have the employees teach me what the numbers meant. People would sit together in teams of four, and each group would be assigned a piece of the P&L. For example, one table group would be assigned the expense category of office supplies. They'd have ten to fifteen minutes to prepare and then they'd present to the entire room how much we spent on office supplies in that category. They'd share whether our spending was going up or down, whether actual spending was within budget or not, what the top items were within the budget. And they'd take questions from the audience. There would be natural times when someone wouldn't understand something, and that gave me the opportunity to teach something about financial fundamentals up at the whiteboard.

Legendary businessman and former CEO of General Electric Jack Welch, in his book *Winning: The Answers*, touts the power of open-book management (Welch and Welch 2006). He writes, "the more information you share with employees about costs and other competitive challenges, the better . . . when people know what they're up against, they can feel a greater sense of ownership and urgency, often sparking homegrown improvements in processes and productivity." But he also warns that employees will also see how much of "the pie" you have, versus how much they have, and that could cause problems.

Personally, I never found that to be the case. In a large company, people who work for you probably already have some sense of what you make for your position in the company, and in fact, that motivates them to be promoted to your level. I've always run small to midsize companies, and I was always careful to separate what was my salary versus profits. And when it came to profits, I taught team members what average profits were for public and private companies, and why investors deserved their returns given the risk versus just putting the money into a stock market index fund.

Speaking of salary information, the original open-book management approach taught leaders to share salary information as a rolled-up total. But what would happen if you shared actual salaries of individual employees?

BUT YOU DON'T SHARE SALARIES, DO YOU?

I returned to my office, after being out on a sales call, where I was leading a team of about fifty people at Kenexa. My assistant pounced when I walked into the lobby. She was pale like she had just seen a ghost. "Do you know?" she asked.

"Know what?"

She whispered, "The email . . ."

I had no idea what she was talking about.

"HR accidentally sent the employee payroll spreadsheet to everyone in the company!"

"How long ago?"

"Like an hour ago. Everyone opened it and is talking about their salaries."

Then it was my turn to look like I had seen a ghost.

I went into my office and pulled up my email in-box. Sure enough, a young woman from HR had sent an "all company" email with the subject line "Employee Salary Spreadsheet" and an attached Excel spreadsheet. Also in my in-box, arriving about five minutes after the salary email was another all-company email from her boss. Subject line: DO NOT OPEN SALARY EMAIL. Obviously everyone ignored the second email and opened the first. I did too. I double-clicked the attachment and sure enough, there was salary information on about five hundred employees. Huh, who knew Bob made $75,000 a year more than I do even though he doesn't have P&L responsibility? I shook it off. I was reacting the way I feared my own team members would. The days ahead were not going to be good.

So you're convinced that radical transparency is the way to lead, right?

Good! So that means you're ready to share salary information with all your employees, too, right?

Yeah, didn't think so.

If you're uncomfortable with sharing salary information, ask yourself, *Why?*

Your knee-jerk reaction is probably: that information is private, it's nobody's business, people would get jealous. The truth?

The reason why I was nervous about everyone seeing one another's salaries back at Kenexa is because I was afraid people would get mad and complain. Or get mad and quit. Neither good. But they'd only get mad if the salary information was unfair. And it probably was because it was totally subjective. It was a black box. Without a salary system, over time, compensation gets out of whack. For example:

- We need to hire our first programmer and after asking around, we are told we should be able to get one for $75,000 per year. So we set that as the average for the role.

- But the candidate we really want says she's making more than that already so we assume we were wrong and pay her $85,000 a year.
- When we go to hire Programmer #2, our desired candidate tells us he's making $65,000 a year. So do we pay him $85,000, the same as Programmer #1? No, we feel like that's too big a jump and want to save some money so we hire him at $72,500.
- When it comes to Programmer #3, we are desperate. Everyone is working around the clock, our clients are mad, we need help! We find someone but she asks for $90,000. We gulp, and pay it.

Before you know it we have three programmers doing roughly the same job but with very different salaries: $72,500, 85,000, and $90,000. And this example doesn't account for the fact that we make mistakes in judging talent. We think we're hiring a supertalented graphic designer but it turns out he's more like an average graphic designer. Do we fire him or insist on a pay cut? No. What about the young gun who comes in untested and at a low salary but is a fast learner, works eighty hours a week, and clients love him. Do we immediately double his pay to reflect his value? No. Even worse would be variations in pay because of conscious or unconscious bias.

The only reason we cringe with the thought of openly sharing salary information is because we fear the reaction of our employees, and the only reason they would react badly is if you have a totally subjective, unfair compensation system. I was guilty as charged.

To get comfortable with the idea of transparent salaries, realize how many people already work that way. All federal workers in the United States are paid according to GS Pay Schedules which consist of fifteen pay grades, and ten steps within each pay grade. Oh, you're a human resources officer in the Department of Justice? That's a GS13 role so that means you make an average of $73,177 before adjustments. Oh, you're a brigadier (one star) general in the US Army? Your rank is also your pay. In the publicly available Military Pay Scale I see that one-stars are paid at the O-7 level which is $8,438.10 per month.

That's government and the military, but did you know all nonprofits in the US have to reveal the compensation of all their top employees? Instead of filing a "tax return," because they don't pay taxes, nonprofits file IRS Form 990. And Part VIII asks for the compensation of all officers, highest-paid employees, and even contractors. And Form 990s are public information and easily located on the internet. This could be fun, let's see . . . the CEO of the National Rifle Association made $1,241,515 in salary plus another $3,810,734 in long-term retirement-related payments (National Rifle Association 2015). The head of the Sierra Club makes $237,622 (Sierra Club 2015).

Even in the private sector, more and more companies are beginning to embrace salary transparency. The belief is that all the millennials talk openly about their paychecks anyway, and with websites like Glassdoor and PayScale, you're only a few clicks from knowing if your current pay is in the ballpark of being fair.

Whole Foods co-CEO John Mackey introduced transparent salaries all the way back in 1986. Any Whole Foods employee can look up the salary of any other employee. In one interview he explained, "If you're trying to create a high-trust organization, an organization where people are all-for-one and one-for-all, you can't have secrets." He says he is indeed challenged by employees about pay discrepancies all the time, and he just explains how the higher-paid employee is providing additional value (Griswold 2014).

While Whole Foods shares their salary information internally, the leaders at software company Basecamp share their compensation system publicly. Basecamp cofounder David Hansson, in a blog post titled "How We Pay People at Basecamp," states, "There are no negotiated salaries or raises at Basecamp. Everyone in the same role at the same level is paid the same. Equal work, equal pay" (Hansson 2017). He goes on to explain that they have five levels of programmers, from junior programmer to principal programmer, with clearly defined role requirements for each level. They determine market rates for each level from an online service and pay at the 95th percentile for each position (but they don't pay bonuses). Market rates are based on Chicago, where their headquarters is, but employees are free to live anywhere they want and the pay isn't adjusted based on geography.

Taking things a step further is the company Buffer, a maker of social media marketing software. Not only do they publicly share their compensation system, they share a spreadsheet showing the salaries of individual employees (last names removed). What's interesting is how different the Buffer system is from the Basecamp system. In a blog post titled, "Introducing the New Buffer Salary Formula, Calculate-Your-Salary App and the Whole Team's New Salaries," they explain that for each role they have a formula composed of:

- Base pay according to location-specific market rates
- A four-level experience multiplier (e.g., if you are a "Master," your base pay is multiplied by 1.3)
- And an addition of $10,000 or stock options (Gascoigne and Widrich 2015)

Each year, rather than haggling over the amount of the annual raise, Buffer gives a 5 percent increase as a "loyalty" factor. On the day I check their salary spreadsheet, the highest-paid employee is Joel, the CEO living in New York City, at $218,000. And the lowest-paid employee is Alfred, Community Champion living in Singapore, at $59,112.

Although the differences in how companies standardize pay are interesting, the point is that having and sharing the system totally changes the conversation with and among the employees. Rather than, "I deserve more" or "I'm worth more than Sue, this is unfair," it becomes a conversation around talent. The question now might be, "You're classifying me as an intermediate programmer and I think I'm a master programmer." The conversation becomes all about skills, accomplishments, and value.

All those years ago when my employees got an email with everyone's salary listed in it I feared the worst. But to my surprise, not a single person came to talk to me about their salary. I'm not naive enough to think that there wasn't some jealousy or even hurt feelings going around. But I'd like to think that while my salary setting was subjective back then, it was still grounded in skill and value.

RADICAL TRANSPARENCY DURING LAYOFFS

I hung up the phone, closed my office door, and put my head in my hands. It was the year 2000 and the dot-com bubble had burst. My partners and I rode the bubble on its way up, building a tech HR company with about $35 million in venture capital; in one year I went from managing about 25 employees to 250. We were growing at all costs and just months away from our initial public offering (IPO) when the NASDAQ began its epic crash. No IPO would be possible for a long time. My CEO called me to say that to survive we had to immediately go from a growth strategy to a cash flow–positive strategy, which meant I would immediately have to lay off a big chunk of my team. Some of the people I would let go had only been hired a couple of months earlier. I pulled the wastebasket closer to me in case I threw up.

How do you communicate to your team, and the outside world, during the worst of times? These days, with the internet and social media, you have to assume that everything you say will be shared with the public. Even if you're addressing your employees, you have to know that your exact word-for-word memo, or email, or speech will be shared with every single customer, partner, and even the media.

When I sat alone in my office that day, I had to think through how many and who to let go, and also how I'd explain it to my remaining team members. I knew that the toughest times were also when radical transparency was most needed. I scribbled down the things I'd want to know if I was in their shoes.

1. What are the facts (e.g., who is affected)?
2. What are the real reasons or causes?
3. Are more cuts coming?
4. What happens next? What does the future look like?

Unfortunately, very few announcements from company leaders address these points. Even fewer address them with clear, plain language. In July of 2014, Microsoft VP Stephen Elop unwittingly became the butt of jokes, and the poster child for how not to communicate layoffs, when he announced that 12,500 employees in his business unit would be let go (if you want to read the entire announcement I've preserved it at kevinkruse.com/bad-layoff-announcement).

The biggest problem with Elop's memo is that it takes him eleven paragraphs and almost a thousand words before he finally says it, "We plan that this would result in an estimated reduction of 12,500 factory direct and professional employees over the next year." Before getting to the main point of the memo, he restates Microsoft strategy, Nokia strategy, market segments, manufacturing locations, and more. Did he think the first eleven paragraphs were going to ease the blow? Did he think the first thousand words would make everyone come to their own conclusion, "Hey, we really need to fire some people around here!"

The second problem with Elop's memo is jargon. Even though Microsoft (and the Nokia division that Elop led) is a technology company, even though everyone there is an experienced business professional, there is no reason not to talk like a human. Plucked from his memo:

- We are the team creating the hardware that showcases the finest of Microsoft's digital work and digital life experiences, and we will be the confluence of the best of Microsoft's applications, operating systems and cloud services.
- Our device strategy must reflect Microsoft's strategy and must be accomplished within an appropriate financial envelope.
- We plan to select the appropriate business model approach for our sales markets while continuing to offer our products in all markets with a strong focus on maintaining business continuity.
- We plan to right-size our manufacturing operations to

align to the new strategy and take advantage of integration opportunities.

Confluence? What the hell is a financial envelope? What does business continuity look like? And the classic, "right size."

If the Microsoft memo is the wrong way to announce layoffs, what's an example of the right way?

Buffer, founded in 2010, offers a tool that helps people to share and schedule their social media marketing posts throughout the day. Although a relatively new and small company, they're beloved by employees and customers alike, which made it especially tough when they announced the layoffs of 11 percent of their workforce in June of 2016. The full announcement can still be found on their website at https://open.buffer.com/layoffs-and-moving-forward/ and I've summarized key points below.

Unlike the Microsoft example, Buffer CEO Joel Gascoigne gets right to the point. Right in the post headline he announces, "Tough News: We've Made 10 Layoffs. How We Got Here, the Financial Details and How We're Moving Forward" (Gascoigne 2016).

Void of jargon, reading the Buffer memo is as if Gascoigne is explaining the situation to you personally over a beer. He opens with:

> The last 3 weeks have been challenging and emotional for everyone at Buffer. We made the hard decision to lay off 10 team members, 11% of the team. I'd like to share the full details of how we got here, and the way we have chosen to handle this situation to put Buffer in a healthier position.

When it comes to the reason for the layoffs, there is no mumbo-jumbo about right-sizing or staying agile or rapidly changing markets. With textbook candor, the CEO put the blame on himself.

> It's the result of the biggest mistake I've made in my career so far. Even worse, this wasn't the result of a market change—it was entirely self-inflicted. . . . The fact is, the challenge that I created has now irrevocably changed people's lives.
>
> Over the course of the last year, Buffer went from 34 to 94 people. . . . Reflecting on it now, I see a lot of ego and pride reflected in that team size number.

And if that isn't honest enough, Gascoigne goes on to list all the other ways they failed: lack of accountability, trust in the financial model, appetite for risk, and team restructuring.

I've never seen company leaders publicly explain their decision making for how they picked the people to be let go. In fact, I've been asked by people I've laid off questions like, "Why did you pick me instead of Dan? Is it because I'm old?" The Buffer blog post actually shares a decision tree—an actual picture of the process—that walks through how they looked at every single role. And if there was an area that had more people than they needed, they chose the employee with the least tenure in what they described as, "a 'last in, first out' approach in order to avoid any bias in selecting individual teammates."

Critically, the announcement also gets specific when it comes to shifting the focus to a more optimistic future. Gascoigne lays out a dozen different changes that will save Buffer money (in addition to the layoffs) and even provides a graph that clearly shows, "We are excited to return to profitability, and I'm confident about the path we're on now. Our bank balance is currently $1.3M, and this will help us grow it back to $2.1M by January 2017." Total transparency with the numbers.

I no longer have the email I sent to my own employees back in 2000. I hope that it was brief, jargon free, and covered four main points:

1. This week we've laid off dozens of our team members; it was the hardest thing I've ever had to do and I'll do everything I can to help them land at another great company.

2. We had to make the cuts because, to drive growth, we were spending more each month than we were bringing in from sales. We anticipated a large cash infusion from an IPO. With the stock market in decline, and no IPO happening, we have to preserve the cash we have left in the bank. We have to operate profitably moving forward.

3. There are no guarantees but we chose to cut deeply now so we won't have to go through this again anytime in the near future.

4. While it's been a painful week, our financials moving forward look strong. [I'd shared revenue, expense, and cash flow projections.] Regardless of what the financial markets do in any given month or year, we are the beginning of a technology revolution and our focus on talent management is the right one. I plan to bring value to our investors, customers, and employees for many decades to come.

THE TAKEAWAY

The hierarchical command-and-control structure, where information flowed up and decisions flowed down, made sense when the world moved at a slower pace. And in that environment, where competing for resources was a zero-sum game, one's individual career could advance by withholding information from others. In today's world marked by VUCA—volatility, uncertainty, complexity, ambiguity—organizations that survive and thrive are the ones that adapt to the changing environment in real time; they push information—including key metrics and financial information—as far forward as possible so frontline workers can make good decisions.

HOW MIGHT YOU APPLY THIS IF YOU'RE A:

MANAGER: Start with the basics. Are team members clear on your annual goals and quarterly objectives? Do they know how much your team's budget is and what the limits are on spending for various areas? Do you share all other metrics that are being tracked for the team and the organization? When it comes to transparency on performance, have you been relentlessly providing feedback on how they can improve and advance in their careers? Have you asked them to critique your performance as a leader?

SALES PROFESSIONAL: Do you have the information you need to reply to customer requests quickly? Do you need to talk to company leadership about the rationale for current pricing, or the true reasons why deliveries are behind schedule? When customers view your business as a black box, they often assume there is much more profit and room to negotiate than there is. Worse, they may see you pull up in an expensive car or see the fancy company headquarters and assume that they are being taken advantage of. Make sure you are as transparent as possible with product costs as well as company profitability and how it compares to industry standards and your competition.

SPORTS COACH: As an athletics coach you will increase the emotional commitment of your players when you are transparent about the "why" of your processes and decisions. Take the time to explain why you have rules about being on time. Explain why you have a dress code or other standards. Explain why you are choosing the drills you are using in a specific practice. When you have to make tough decisions—who's your starting quarterback, who is going to make the team—explain your rationale.

MILITARY OFFICER: Trust is the intangible bedrock for success in the military: trust between troops, trust between soldiers and their leaders, trust between the military force and their nation. As a military leader, you must model and encourage transparent values-based decision making, encourage transparency by viewing many mistakes as learning opportunities, and share as much information as possible so that frontline troops are able to make strategic decisions.

PARENT: Being radically transparent as a parent can be tricky. We want our children to respect us, and we don't want to accidentally encourage bad choices by letting them know about our bad behaviors when we were their age. But most families err on the side of withholding too much information. When my teenage daughters began to drive, I made sure to tell them about the two auto accidents I had that, while technically not my fault, I knew I had contributed to. Many illnesses including depression have a genetic component and our grown children would benefit from knowing what ails their parents and grandparents. If you want your kids to understand the value of money, perhaps you should share your monthly bills. If you want to encourage them to get a well-paying job, let them know how much you've made in different jobs throughout your career. If you want your children to feel comfortable coming to you in their times of crisis, they need to know that you can relate, and that you may have made similar mistakes to the ones they have made.

INDIVIDUAL: With friends, siblings, and spouses it's always easier to just brush things off that are bothering us. It's sometimes easier to keep things a secret than to explain the truth ("Uhm, yes, that was my ex-girlfriend who texted me"). Well, it's easier in the short term. The problem is that little things don't disappear; we just hold on to them and carry them with us, eventually blasting them out during some other disagreement. And of course your friends and family aren't mind readers, or feelings readers either. When you are upset about something, try using this phrase to start the conversation. "I feel _____, when you _____."

B randon Brooks was looking forward to the game. As a six-foot-five, 340-pound offensive lineman in the NFL, his job was to stop opponents from sacking his quarterback, and to open up holes for his running backs. It was his first year playing for the Philadelphia Eagles, who signed him to a $40 million five-year contract the previous summer. That comes out to half a million dollars per game. And this wasn't going to be just any game, it was *Monday Night Football*. For the players it's a chance to strut their stuff in front of a nationwide, even global, audience.

This particular Monday, the Eagles were to face off against the Green Bay Packers. Although both teams were struggling throughout the season, they were still fighting against long odds for a playoff spot, and of course for pride. Nobody wants to look bad in front of ten million viewers on live TV.

On game day, at five in the morning, Brooks woke up, rushed to the bathroom, and threw up violently. It felt like he had stomach flu. He got himself to the Eagles stadium, but despite team doctors' best efforts, instead of suiting up for *Monday Night Football*, Brooks went to the hospital. The Eagles lost to Green Bay 13–27.

Two weeks later it happened again. After feeling fine all week in practice, on game day, at five in the morning, Brooks experienced uncontrollable vomiting. Too weak to even stand, this time he would miss the Eagles game against division rival the Washington Redskins. Fans and sports reporters alike wondered, *What is his mysterious illness?* Three days later, standing in front of his locker surrounded by the media, Brooks talked about his condition:

> I found out recently that I have an anxiety condition. . . . I have like an obsession with the game. It's an unhealthy obsession right now and I'm working with team doctors to get everything straightened out and getting the help that I need and things like that. For me, it's just I always want to be perfect in what I do and if I'm not perfect it's not good enough, and sometimes that just really weighs on you. And I have to learn how to kind of chill out and understand it's OK to make mistakes. It's OK to not be perfect (Frank 2016).

I had a chance to have dinner with Brooks about a year after his impromptu press conference. He told me that before he knew he had an anxiety condition, his goal was to be perfect. Literally. He said,

My goal was to not give up a single sack for the entire season. That's all I thought about. Before the game my mind would race through all the scenarios against whoever I'd be up against. If he moves his left foot out, where will I move? If he moves here, I have to move there. After the game, if I had one bad play, that's all I'd think about. I'd replay it over and over (Brooks 2017).

He said signing the big contract with the Eagles amplified his emotions; he feared failure because he didn't want to let anyone down. Brooks now sees a psychologist each week and has been exploring the roots of condition. It's hard to describe but listening to Brooks talk, I could tell he was just as driven to win and driven to be great as ever, but somehow the pressure was off. He said he now realizes that he can't control everything that happens in the game, knows mistakes will happen, and when they do it won't be the end of the world.

Brooks told me he had no hesitation about coming out publicly about his anxiety. He doesn't pay attention to the haters on social media, and all the Eagles coaches and players have been supportive. Since letting go of the need to be perfect, and by openly sharing his struggle, Brooks has emerged stronger than ever before. Little did we know at the time of our dinner, but Brooks didn't miss a single game of the 2017 season, he was nominated to the Pro Bowl, and the Eagles would go on to win the Super Bowl LII.

THE NEED TO OUTRUN THE LION

"Will you tell me about a time when you failed?"

It's the first question I ask of all my guests on *The LEADx Leadership Show.* From Dan Pink to Captain Sully Sullenberger to Alan Alda, from bestselling authors to entrepreneurs and big company CEOs. When have you failed and what did you learn from it?

My guests invariably chuckle nervously and stall with some kind of joke like, "Wow, there have been so many times it's hard to pick just one!" And then they give me something real. Something they've never talked about in an interview, and often a story they've never even told friends or colleagues. Listeners of the show tell me all the time this is their favorite question, because to hear a supersuccessful person talk about anything other than their achievements is so rare.

In one survey of over 210,000 business leaders, 43 percent indicated they "have no problem being seen as vulnerable." This leaves over half who have some kind of problem with vulnerability (Figliuolo 2017).

Why do we instinctively hide our weaknesses? Anyone who's ever watched the Discovery Channel knows there's an evolutionary component. Nothing good ever happens to the slowest gazelle. Today, we might not have to outrun a hungry lion—or more accurately, outrun one of our friends—but we still learn early lessons about what happens to the weak. Our parents may give not-so-subtle signals like "suck it up" or "stop being a baby." In grade school we get picked last for the dodge-ball team, in high school we get cut from basketball, and we get bullied throughout. Socially our instinct is to do everything we can to fit in; we'll do almost anything to avoid the shame and pain of failing. If the herd rejects us, well, we're back to that hungry lion.

At work, at least traditionally, we were penalized for our "weaknesses," too. If we make a mistake, we're liable to be reprimanded. If we reveal that we're sick, or that we're dealing with an ailing parent, or that we're getting a divorce, suddenly our ability to put in long hours gets questioned. If we don't know something, we get judged by those who overvalue domain expertise. And let's face it, a big part of "executive presence" is a display of confidence.

So why should we suddenly go against two hundred thousand years of modern humans' evolutionary biology and social constructs to suddenly share our weaknesses?

THE JUNGLE HAS CHANGED; WE SHOULD TOO

We no longer live in the jungle; we are not at risk from the lion. Neither literally, nor metaphorically. The world of work has changed and behaviors that worked through the industrial revolution have now become liabilities. Vulnerability is the key to thriving in the new environment.

VULNERABILITY BUILDS TRUST. We no longer operate in a hierarchical command-and-control structure where power and authority are the keys to getting things done. Today it's all about relationships, social capital, and, to borrow a term from General Stanley McChrystal, building a "team of teams." Trust is often called the lubrication of relationships. Indeed, neuroscientist Paul Zak has conducted research on trust in the workplace and found that in organizations high in trust, people collaborate more effectively with their colleagues, are more productive, and they stay in their jobs longer (Zak 2017). If you think about your most trusted friends, invariably they're the ones you can tell anything to. So when someone at work reveals a weakness or some kind of fault or shortcoming, we can't help but trust them a bit more than before. Who tells us their weaknesses? Our closest friends! Zak's research shows that trust is reciprocal; the more you trust me, the more I trust you, and a virtuous cycle begins.

VULNERABILITY INCREASES EMPLOYEE ENGAGEMENT. Vulnerability builds trust, and trust is one of the top three drivers of engagement, which is the emotional commitment employees have for their organization and its goals. When we're engaged, we care. And when we care, we release discretionary effort and we're more likely to stay in our companies longer.

Our parents or grandparents looked forward to working at one company throughout their entire career. Today, we can (and do) find new jobs with the click of the mouse. The reality is that the most talented workers also have the most opportunities for employment elsewhere. Great leaders care about their connection with their direct reports, and a great connection begins by showing your weakness.

VULNERABILITY DRIVES INNOVATION. The new world of work is so crazy someone had to come up with an acronym to describe it: VUCA. Volatile, uncertain, complex, and ambiguous. Technology innovation is accelerating exponentially, leaving formerly great companies behind. According to McKinsey, the average lifespan of a Fortune 500 company in 1935 was ninety years; today it's just eighteen years (Borpuzari 2016). There is only one way for an organization to survive, and that's through endless rapid innovation. And innovation requires a lot of failure.

Entrepreneurs more naturally understand this idea and often preach "fail fast." While nobody intentionally sets out to fail, there is an understanding that innovation requires a lot of experiments, most of which won't work out. But after each "failure" you learn and adapt and try again. Great leaders know they must model the way and share their own failures—and celebrate the smart failures of others—to build a culture of effective risk-taking. I often say, "There is no win or lose, only win or learn."

BEING VULNERABLE IS HEALTHY. Let's be real, it's just easier and less stressful to live authentically. It takes courage, but requires less energy. Vulnerability researcher Brené Brown reports that perfectionism strongly correlates to increases in anxiety, depression, and substance abuse.

"Perfectionism is a twenty-ton shield that we lug around, thinking it will protect us, when in fact it's the thing that's really preventing us from being seen. . . . Perfectionism is, at its core, about trying to earn approval. . . . Healthy striving is self-focused: How can I improve? Perfectionism is other-focused: What will they think?" (Schawbel 2013).

If a 340-pound professional football player can literally be felled by his need for perfection, you can be certain that the stress you are carrying around is taking a toll as well.

WHEN YOU FALL DOWN, I LIKE YOU BETTER

My friend Christine is a great presenter, and also a very nervous one. At one conference, right before her speech, she came to me visibly stressed. I tried to make her feel better by asking, "What's the worst that can happen?"

She pointed down to her high heel shoes. "I don't know, I could fall down!"

The conference host read Christine's introduction and then loudly in the microphone, "Please welcome, Christine MacAdams."

The audience applauded and as Christine got to the second step of the stage, yes, she tripped and fell down. And that was the moment she won the audience over.

Social psychologists call it the pratfall effect. It's the tendency for people to like—even to be more attracted to—an individual who makes a mistake. In most studies this effect only applies when the person making the blunder is viewed by others as socially superior. An inept person making a blunder would just be viewed as, well, still inept.

The term "pratfall effect" was coined by social psychologist Elliot Aronson in 1966 to describe the results of his study looking at how we view people after they make a "blunder." He recruited college students who were told they would be listening to a tape recording of a student who is trying out for the college "quiz bowl" competition. The recorded contestant was asked fifty questions, but in half the recordings, the contestant spilled a cup of coffee and could be heard saying, "Oh my goodness, I've spilled coffee all over my new suit." (If that language seems implausible, remember, this was 1966.) Afterward the study participants were asked a variety of questions to gauge how well they liked the quiz bowl contestant. It turns out, the blunder of spilling the coffee increased likability by 45 percent. Aronson explained, "a superior person may be viewed as superhuman and, therefore, distant; a blunder tends to humanize him and, consequently, increases his attractiveness" (Aronson, Willerman, and Floyd 1966).

The pratfall effect is so powerful that people even like robots better when they make mistakes. European researchers studying the new field of social robotics gathered almost fifty college students and a two-foot-tall humanoid robot. The participants were split into two groups. In each group, the robot asked questions and then gave instructions on how to use toy blocks to build simple structures. In one group the robot performed flawlessly, and in the other group the robot was programmed to make mistakes. It turns out, both groups rated their robot the same in intelligence (i.e., making mistakes didn't make people think it was less smart) but the robot that made mistakes was viewed as more likable (Mirnig et al. 2017).

Do your team members put you on a pedestal? Show them you're human for a better connection.

THE HERO'S JOURNEY

Standing in front of three hundred people, I knew I bombed again. All that preparation, all the rehearsing, and all I got was a polite golf clap. That is, from the people who weren't asleep. I walked off the stage embarrassed and disappointed that my message wasn't having an impact.

Why weren't they more interested? Didn't they know what I had accomplished? I'm an Inc. 500 award-winning entrepreneur. I won a Best Place to Work in PA award for great workplace culture. I built a business from $0 to $12 million in revenue in four years and then sold it in a big exit. And let's not forget I'm a hotshot *New York Times* bestselling author!

But after my sixty minutes, the truth was undeniable. *Clap. Clap. Clap.*

I knew I had to make a change. If I wanted to help more people, I'd need to learn how to be more effective as a communicator. I paid a ridiculous amount of money for one of the world's top public speakers to personally coach me. I read dozens of books not just on public speaking, but on persuasion and psychology. I wrote and rewrote my speech two dozen times. I began to study stand-up comedians not for the jokes but for their timing.

My number-one takeaway after all this work was: people want to learn from people they can relate to. People *trust* people who openly share their weaknesses, their failures.

So I began to open my speeches by talking about my business failures. How I had to lay off 30 percent of my employees. How I was such a jerk-boss that one employee actually threatened to beat me up. How I was once demoted. And then I shared how I changed. What I did differently that then led to the award-winning companies and multimillion-dollar company sales.

With this change, the audience leaned in. They asked questions. They clapped loudly. And every now and then, I get a standing ovation.

FRIENDS, I JUST hit you with a "hero's journey" story to make a point. It's all true. I did stink as a speaker and now I'm pretty darned good. But I told the story in a particular way. I opened the story in a particular way. And if I were a betting man, I'd wager that you were hooked by the first couple of sentences, curious about how I got better, and you felt happy for me that I was suddenly getting standing ovations.

The hero's journey is a term that refers to a classic storytelling structure that goes back for centuries. The idea has been popularized by Joseph Campbell in his 1949 book, *The Hero with a Thousand Faces*, and PBS's 1978 documentary *The Hero's Journey: The World of Joseph Campbell*. Campbell details seventeen different stages of a typical hero's journey story, which includes the call to adventure, crossing the threshold, and even unusual things like "woman as temptress" and "atonement with the father" (Campbell 1973). Others have summarized it in a variety of ways, and my own simplification of the monomyth is simply as follows:

- Act I: Hero is in trouble and forced on an adventure
- Act II: Hero overcomes problems with the help of new allies/friends and special objects/weapons

- Act III: Hero defeats the enemy and wins, only because she is transformed by the trials and tribulations of Act II

You can see these patterns in the works of Melville, Dickens, Faulkner, Hemingway, Twain, Tolkien, Stephen King, and so many others. Hollywood taps into this centuries-old winning formula over and over again. Think of *The Wizard of Oz, Harry Potter, The Lion King,* and definitely *Star Wars.* You could tell almost the same story simply by changing the character and setting.

Star Wars opens with an attack on a ship carrying Princess Leia, who sends R2D2 off to recruit a reluctant Luke Skywalker. Luke is just a kid with no game whatsoever. But with the help of new friends (primarily Obi-Wan Kenobi and Yoda) and some new tools (a light saber and the Force) Luke is transformed into a Jedi who destroys the death star. He and his friends are celebrated.

So what does *Star Wars* have in common with, say, the *Wizard of Oz*?

The *Wizard of Oz* begins with a disgruntled teenager, Dorothy, being forced by a tornado into a new, colorful but dangerous world. She sets off on a literal road of adventure attracting new allies and friends (Glinda the good witch, the Tin Man, the Cowardly Lion, and the Scarecrow) and getting some new tools (ruby slippers). Now transformed, Dorothy is able to defeat the bad witch, confront the Wizard, and return home where everyone is happy.

Now go back and read the story at the beginning of this section, about how I used to be bad at public speaking. It's okay, I'll wait . . .

Ahh, now you see what I did right? I pulled a hero's journey structure:

- ACT I: Kevin is so horrible at speaking he's embarrassed and in pain
- ACT II: Kevin hires a speaking coach, gets books, and is transformed
- ACT III: Kevin battles the audience again but this time wins the day with a standing ovation

It might not seem like a very important trick, but consider all the other ways I could have started this section of the book. In earlier drafts I started with:

- "The hero's journey refers to a recurring storytelling structure . . ."
- "In 1949, a man by the name of Joseph Campbell . . ."
- "Great leaders tap into the power of heroic myths . . ."

Bleh. Actually diving in, using the hero's journey, is the right way to go.

And if you're not quite sure what this has to do with leadership, just remember you are communicating *all the time.* The hero's journey works perfectly if you ever have to give a speech. It also works if you have to give a big internal presentation. And it even works, if you don't overuse it, when you are just communicating with your own team members. The key is to openly share your weaknesses and failures—remember the pratfall effect—and explain how you overcame them.

And don't think your stories have to always be two hours long. You're not actually Luke or Dorothy. You could tell a story in as little as three sentences. Let's look at some examples.

You can lead with weakness and use the hero's journey in times of crisis.

> Ten years ago the stress was unbelievable. . . . I had made a mistake and we were in a bad cash flow crisis. But our CFO renegotiated payment terms with our best suppliers, a new banking partner expanded our borrowing line, and our employees rallied by moving invoices out the door faster and finding ways to spend a little less. In less than six months we returned to being cash positive and . . .

You can lead with weakness and use the hero's journey to coach and develop your team members.

> I remember almost getting fired when I was in the field as a sales rep because the biggest buyer in the country was in my territory, but I couldn't get them to buy anything. Finally I got advice from a senior rep who said, "People buy from people they like." I went back in to that prospect and instead of features and benefits, I asked about his kids, his alma mater, and his favorite sports teams. It took a while but eventually I cracked that account open and a couple years later they were our biggest customer.

You can lead with weakness and use the hero's journey when you have a new job.

> It's true, I'm not going to lie, I have no experience and know nothing about the biotech industry. And when I started at Acme ten years ago, I didn't know anything about managing software engineers. Back then I got one of the senior guys to mentor me for an hour a day, I sat down one-on-one

to learn what everyone did, and I networked with my peers in other companies to learn from their experiences. It took a while, but at my going-away party last week they all said I had become one of them . . .

We are wired to respond to the hero's journey. It works in books, movies, and in real life. We cheer for the hero, we want her to win. But, remember, that's only true if we can relate to them first. We need to know they're human, that they make mistakes, just like everyone else.

FROM VULNERABILITY TO TMI

Despite all that I had to gain from being a more vulnerable leader, early in my journey I couldn't help but wonder, *Is there such a thing as too much information or oversharing as an authentic leader?*

For example, I once panicked many employees by sharing the fact that we were losing money, even though we were beating our budget and had several years' worth of runway left in the bank. Should I have held that fact back?

I decided to call up my friend Randy Hetrick, a former Navy SEAL officer and founder and CEO of TRX, a company that makes suspension fitness equipment. Given his success in both the military and the private sector, I thought he'd have a unique point of view. He explained that radical transparency is the best approach, *if* your team members can handle it. He said:

> As a SEAL Team officer, I made a point to always be forthright and truthful with my guys. The activities we were involved in might literally kill you if things went wrong. Given that, I believed that all teammates were owed the full

score, not some edited version of the details. SEALs want and expect that from their leaders, and they're equipped to deal with it.

Even in the SEAL community, a leader must learn to moderate and modulate the less-rational, more emotional fears that all humans face. If there is a significant, fact-based misgiving, then the leader needs to stop the training and address it. But if it is just one's own internal anxieties, the leader's job is to manage them and to project the confidence that a well-trained team deserves to rally around (Hetrick 2016).

Don't use Hetrick's advice as an excuse not to share. The responsibility falls on you to ensure your team members "are equipped to deal with it." Going back to my personal example, if my profit-loss data frightened some team members, it's a sure sign that they either didn't truly understand basic financial principles or they didn't recall what our objectives for the quarter were. Yes, they should take ownership over these things. But as their leader it should have signaled me to increase my efforts around strategic alignment and understanding financials for everyone.

More instructive to me was the second part of Hetrick's lesson. A leader still needs to project confidence, so irrational emotions that would be counter to that goal should *not* be shared. You can still talk about your own shortcomings and limitations, because as Hetrick told me, "Your teams will appreciate the candor and humility and, hell, they'll sniff them out anyway!" But when it comes to fears, business leaders should focus on the plan and their faith in their colleagues to embrace an optimistic view of the future.

If you're ever in doubt about whether your attempts at self-disclosure are going to do more harm than good, consider these questions before you possibly overshare.

1. **What is your intent?** Carefully consider, are you sharing to be helpful, to teach, or to build trust? Or are you just being needy? Is the real reason behind your disclosures a personal need to vent, to complain, to get attention, or driven by your need to have friends in the workplace?

2. **Are they equipped to handle radical transparency?** Do they understand what success looks like? What the organization's goals are? Are they mature enough to know that there are always risks in any venture? Do they have the confidence in the team to move forward productively into an uncertain future?

3. **How close is the relationship?** One way to modulate your transparency is to be more open with those who are closest to you, and share less with those who are more distant. If you're a business owner facing a dire financial situation, maybe your direct reports—the CFO and your VPs—get total transparency and you admit that you're worried and don't have any ideas. After all, you'll need their help to come up with solutions and they should have the experience to handle it. But maybe their direct reports are told of the situation, but with less detail and less emotional honesty.

4. **Will it violate the trust of anyone else?** One easy transparency screen is just asking if your radical transparency will violate the privacy of or embarrass anyone else. Embracing authenticity and transparency doesn't give you license to gossip or to talk about people behind their back. I've always admired the investor, author, and pod-

caster James Altucher. He is the most transparent public figure I know. He frequently talks about his worst moments, from stalking girlfriends and suicide attempts, to going broke and getting divorced. But never once has he ever said one thing about his ex-wives or former business partners. When in doubt, leave them out.

THE TAKEAWAY

Sharing your weaknesses, mistakes, and failures—your pratfalls—will help you to build trust, engage your team members, and foster a culture of innovation. But don't use it in a contrived or manipulative way. That's an inauthentic way of being authentic. Great leaders know how to drop the masks and just be the best version of their unique selves. They know that showing weakness actually is the strongest sign of courage and confidence.

HOW MIGHT YOU APPLY THIS IF YOU'RE A:

MANAGER: Building trust, increasing engagement, and fostering a culture that fuels innovation is as easy as showing more of the real you. Take advantage of all the times you can answer, "I have no idea, but I'll find out for you." Or, "We missed our quarterly goal, and ultimately it's my fault." You'll improve your own performance when you spend time on self-awareness so you can lean into your strengths and hire for your weaknesses.

SALES PROFESSIONAL: My favorite Christmas movie is the 1947 classic *Miracle on 34th Street*. In one scene the Macy's Santa Claus tells a shocked customer to go to rival Gimbels department store to get a toy that Macy's didn't carry. This unexpected gesture generates a ton of goodwill and publicity for Macy's. I always tell my salespeople they should look for opportunities to say no, to turn down projects, and especially to say no to demands for lower fees. When your prospects hear you admit that you are not the right partner for them, you dramatically increase trust and credibility (rare commodities in sales unfortunately). This is so powerful that I've often opened my own sales calls with a proactive no in the form of, "If you're looking for _____, we aren't for you. But if you want _____, then we are the best on the planet."

SPORTS COACH: Red-faced, screaming at the top of their lungs—I've seen so many coaches of youth sports instill fear and stress in boys and girls. Your goal should be to get your players to strive to be their best, not to be perfect. You want to teach them to flush away any mistakes they make because the most important play is always the next play. When you share your own mistakes—whether from your own childhood sports experiences or something later—you will earn the trust and respect of your players. They'll play harder for you and will deal with their own mistakes in the most appropriate ways.

MILITARY OFFICER: More than any other organization, military forces around the world develop and reward toughness and mission results. This is with good reason given what is at stake. But there are times when confidence and strength are exhibited by revealing a mistake or asking for help. Whether it's sharing a tactical failure to help develop a young officer, or seeking help for hearing loss or PTSD, you can perform better when you show authenticity and vulnerability.

PARENT: You can raise resilient children by sharing all the times you've made mistakes and failed, but got back up and found success again. If you talk about your personal weaknesses in addition to what you do well, you are giving a positive lesson about self-awareness and how to lean into your strengths. And if you want your kids to turn to you in their toughest times, they'll be more likely to feel comfortable doing so if they know you faced similar circumstances.

INDIVIDUAL: We all display different facets of our personality at different times or in different settings. But do you frequently wear a mask? Are you uncomfortable sharing your mistakes, failures, and weaknesses? Think about the way you were raised . . . did you get love and praise for what you accomplished, rather than for effort or for who you are? Your own desire for perfection may be taking a toll on your health and is likely putting a distance between you and those around you. Look for opportunities to share the real you, including your fears and limitations, with those closest to you. Look for opportunities at work to gain trust by sharing mistakes.

LEADERSHIP IS NOT A CHOICE

In the late 1800s, there was an unusual French-man named Gustave Le Bon. I say unusual because he was trained as a doctor but traveled the world as an anthropologist (he was the first French-man to visit Nepal), conducted research as a physicist (he was nominated for the Nobel Prize), and wrote extensively on psychology. I also say he was unusual because as a "craniologist" he invented a device so he could measure the skulls of women who he believed "represent the most inferior forms of human evolution and . . . are closer to children and savages than to an adult civilized man" (Le Bon 2002). Yikes!

If we can get past the misogyny, we have to give Le Bon credit for writing a book that would inspire dictators, launch a field of psychology, and some would say even predict the rise of Trump and viral cat memes on the internet. In *The Crowd: A Study of the Popular Mind*, first published in 1895, Le Bon lays out the first detailed analysis of crowd psychology. He is the first to formulate the theory of social contagion (he used the word *contagion* thirty times in one hundred pages), describing how emotions, ideas, and behaviors spread from person to person like a virus. The phenomenon of social contagion is why I say leadership is not a choice.

Leadership, with its endless definitions, is most often boiled down to one word: *influence*. I was having lunch with leadership guru Ken Blanchard when I asked him, "If you had to define leadership in a single word, what would it be?" Without hesitation Blanchard answered, "Influence." Speaker, author, and leadership expert John Maxwell often says, "Leadership is influence—nothing more, nothing less" (Maxwell 2016). In his book *Leadership for the Twenty-First Century*, Professor Joseph Rost reviews the changing definitions of leadership over seven centuries and concludes that the through-line is, "Leadership is an influence relationship" (Rost 1993).

In this chapter you'll discover that because of social contagion you influence people all the time, even without trying. Even if you don't want to. You even influence strangers. You influence others when you act, and when you stand by. You influence others when you speak up, and when you remain silent. And because influence = leadership, this means leadership is not a choice. You're leading whether you want to or not.

LEADERSHIP AND SEX, DRUGS, AND ROCK 'N' ROLL

While most smokers and nonsmokers alike are probably well aware of the dangers of secondhand smoke, most probably don't realize that secondhand smoke can lead to firsthand addiction.

Researchers at the University of Washington, Seattle, asked 808 fifth graders about their smoking habits, and the habits of their parents (Hill et al. 2005). They were surveyed again several times for seven years. After controlling for demographics and other factors, the analysis concluded that children whose parents smoked were twice as likely to begin smoking by the age of twenty-one than kids who had nonsmoking parents. What didn't matter was the parents' own attitudes toward smoking. Mom and Dad could tell their kids it's a dirty, expensive habit and that they wish they could quit, but it didn't matter.

But there's good news for all you parents who just decided to quit to save not your own health, but the health of your kids. It turns out social influence works in the other direction, too. Quitting smoking is also contagious. Nicholas Christakis of Harvard Medical School and James Fowler at the University of California San Diego analyzed three decades of health information from twelve thousand individuals and their social networks (Christakis and Fowler 2008). They discovered that when one person quit smoking, their immediate friends and family members were 36 percent less likely to remain smokers. And even friends of friends were 20 percent less likely to smoke. The researchers summarized their findings, "People appeared to act under collective pressures within niches in the network."

THEY'LL HAVE WHAT YOU'RE HAVING

Not every university has its own fake bar, but the Behavioural Science Institute of Radboud University in the Netherlands has just that. The Bar Lab, as it's called, looks like a normal bar or pub and even has a working beer tap. But it also has a network of sophisticated cameras and microphones that record individuals' social interactions during behavioral experiments.

It was in this lab that researchers studied the effect of social contagion on how much we eat when we're among others. (Hermans, Larsen, et al. 2012). They invited eighty-five first-year women to participate in an experiment, and as is common in behavioral research, they were lied to (it was only a white lie). Each female participant was told the experiment had to do with nutrition and cognitive function. She would have to play games on a Nintendo Wii to measure brain function, then she would eat a meal with another woman and take some more cognitive tests. Of course, the Wii games were just a cover and had nothing to do with the experiment.

The real experiment took place in the Bar Lab. The participants were paired up and sat at a table for two where they ordered from a menu of lasagna, macaroni, spaghetti, or a Dutch meal called stamppot (Google tells me this is combination of mashed potatoes and vegetables). And one of the two women at the table was secretly a confederate who was working for the scientists. One-third of the time the confederate was told to eat a standard amount of food; in another third of the experiments, the confederate was told to eat a small amount of food (half a standard portion); and in a final third of the experiments, the confederate was told to eat a large amount of food (50 percent more than a standard size). And the portions were actually marked off with secret lines on their plates.

What the researchers found was that, after controlling for a variety of other variables, the participants ate about 10 percent less if their dining partner ate less, and they ate about 10 percent more if their partner ate more. And these researchers did something else (remember the cameras!). They actually watched and recorded every single bite of food of all the study pairs—3,888 bites in all. In what psychologists call behavioral mimicry, instead of eating at their own random pace, the women tended to mirror each other's eating pattern, each taking a bite of food within five seconds of the other person taking a bite of food (Hermans, Litchtwarck-Aschoff, et al. 2012).

Another study, this one taking place in an actual working restaurant, used sales receipts from 1,532 customers to uncover peer influence patterns in making decisions about what to eat (Ellison 2014). The menu contained fifty-one different items, in eight separate categories (e.g., salads, entrées, specials). Using a variety of statistical tools, the researchers found that people eating in groups tended to choose different items, but within the same groups. For example, if we were eating together and you ordered a chicken-salad sandwich, I would be less likely to also order a chicken-salad sandwich, but more likely to order the tuna sandwich, as opposed to say, the meatloaf special. As the researchers wrote, "it would appear diners want to be different from their peers but not too different."

In another example of how our actions influence those around us—whether we want them to or not—how and what we eat impacts the food consumption of those we're eating with.

LEADING YOUR KIDS

Ask your teenage child, "How would you rate our communication, on a scale from one to ten, with one being 'very poor' and ten being 'excellent'?" Researchers in Madison, Wisconsin, asked teens this question and the average score was 7.5 (mothers tend to get scored higher, and fathers lower; sorry, dads) (Karofsky, Zeng, and Kosorok 2001). That was just one question that was asked in a ten-year longitudinal study of over two hundred adolescents. Each year the participants were asked again a variety of questions about their sexual activity, drugs and alcohol, school, family, and specifically about the quality of their communication with parents.

They found that on average teens lost their virginity at 15.1 years of age. And as every year went by—as the teens became one year older—the odds that they lost their virginity went up significantly (odds ratio of 1.7). What could bring these results back down? In other words, what could delay teens from becoming sexually active? Communication with their parents. In fact, for every 10 percent improvement in parental communication—in other words, your teen increases your score from 7.5 to 8.5—the odds of sexual activity decreased by almost half (odds ratio = 0.649). So did you get your score from your own teenager? Now ask them, what would it take to increase that number by one?

When it comes to "safe sex," a study of 5,461 high school freshmen showed a strong correlation between parents talking to their kids about sexual risks and the teens' use of a condom the first time they had sex (odds ratio = 2.05) (Atienzo et al. 2009). Other similar studies have shown even stronger correlations. This metric is especially critical because teens who use condoms when they lose their virginity are twenty times more likely to continue using them (Miller et al. 1998).

In my own layman's terms, what all these studies loosely suggest is:

- If you talk to your teenagers about safe sex, they are twice as likely use a condom.
- If you don't talk to teens about safe sex, they are half as likely to use a condom.

You have a choice as a parent. It's awkward, I know. You can talk to your kids about abstinence and safe sex, or you can assume the school has it covered, or your kids are just "good kids." Know that with your decision you are influencing your kids in one direction, or another.

LEADING AT THE DINNER TABLE

Eating dinner together as a family is a great way for parents to connect with their children, monitor their kids' activities and moods, and to explicitly or implicitly offer life lessons or other guidance. And in 1998, researchers from the University of Minnesota set out to determine if this family practice actually reduces the odds of substance abuse in teenagers. So they surveyed 806 middle-school students, asking them questions related to family connectedness and how often they used cigarettes, alcohol, and marijuana (Sen 2010). Of note was the question, "During the past seven days, how many times did all or most of your family living in your house eat a meal together?" The researchers chose five or more meals per week to represent "regular family meals."

Previous studies indeed showed negative correlations between family dinners and substance abuse, but these studies were only single snapshots in time. Correlation is not causation, after all. Perhaps it wasn't that family dinners led to less drug use, but maybe kids who were on drugs were skipping out on the family meals so they wouldn't get caught.

So the researchers in Minnesota actually resurveyed the same kids five years later, who were then about seventeen years old. This longitudinal study also controlled for factors like gender, race, and socioeconomic status. What they found was fascinating. Indeed, teenage girls were half as likely to report using cigarettes, alcohol, or marijuana in high school if their family regularly ate dinner together. (Interestingly, there was no correlation with the teenage boys. The researchers theorized that females are more likely than males to pick up on emotional support offered during the meals.) In 2010, another study looked more closely at the gender difference and found that the effect of meals was the same, but the undesired behavior males exhibited was different—most notably fighting and property destruction (Eisenberg et al. 2008).

This data is compelling even if it only applies to our daughters. Once again, leadership as a parent is not a choice. Your family practice is influential one way or the other:

- If you regularly eat dinner as a family, your daughters are half as likely to abuse substances in high school.
- If you don't regularly eat dinner as a family, your daughters are twice as likely to abuse substances in high school.

A similar study looked at family dinners and a wider range of high-risk behaviors among teens. In one of the largest studies ever conducted with teens, researchers collected anonymous surveys from 99,462 students, in 213 different cities, in twenty-five states across the US (Fulkerson et al., 2006). Once again researchers controlled for things like family support and communication and even intrinsic motivation, to better isolate the effect of family dinners. In this particular study, there was correlation between family dinners and substance abuse in both females and males. Additionally, there was strong correlation between frequency of family dinners and teens being sexually active. In families that had dinner together five to seven times a week, 11.8 percent of teen children reported being sexually active. But that number increases to 20 percent and 30.2 percent in families that eat together two to four times, and zero to one times per week, respectively.

Once again, we see that parents are leading in one direction or another.

- If you regularly eat dinner as a family, your teenage children are one-third as likely to be sexually active.
- If you don't regularly eat dinner as a family, your teenage children are three times more likely to be sexually active.

One thing I was immediately curious about was the effect of watching TV while having a family dinner. I'm pretty sure I've seen every episode of *M.A.S.H.* and the original *Star Trek* series because as a kid my family would routinely eat in the living room using those metal foldout TV trays. I was only able to find one study that addressed this, and to my surprise TV viewing made no difference on the positive effect of families eating dinner together (Eisenberg, Neumark-Sztainer, and Feldman 2009).

OTHER CRAZY WAYS YOU LEAD OTHERS AROUND YOU

Ten years ago I was running my fifty-person company, AXIOM, from a corner office. And I got divorced. At the time I didn't personally know a single person who had been divorced. I was the first. And at work sitting within fifty feet of my office were about ten employees, mostly people I managed directly. I assumed all were happily married. Then Sarah got divorced. Soon after, Cynthia did, too. Then I got an email out of the blue from Stephanie, "Kevin, I know this is random but can you recommend a good divorce attorney?" Mindy got divorced next. Karen, who upon hearing of my own breakup told me she would never in a million years leave her husband, apparently changed her mind a little sooner than that. It took longer, but eventually Mark got divorced, too. (Or course I've changed all their names.) Within a couple years of me getting a divorce, over half the people who worked in that corner of the office—nearest to me—got divorced. A statistical coincidence or something else?

In 2013, researchers Rose McDermott, James Fowler, and Nicholas Christakis published the results of a study and made headlines around the world (McDermott, Fowler, and Christakis 2013). The trio analyzed three decades' worth of marriage and divorce data, along with social connections, and discovered what they called "divorce clusters." They concluded that "divorce can spread between friends" and even extends to degrees of separation in a social network. Statistically speaking, they determined that when a friend ends their marriage, the odds of your own marital split increases by 75 percent. And, when a coworker gets divorced, the odds of you getting a divorce goes up by 55 percent.

While others have shed doubt about the statistical methods used in this study, nobody doubts that there is some amount of peer effect going on. Is it possible that my divorce news suddenly made those around me think about it in their own life? When they saw that I was actually happier than ever before, and that my kids were doing great, did that provide some kind of psychological encouragement? I'll never know for sure, and I have no regrets, but I do have to assume that my decision to divorce led (i.e., influenced) those around me a little further down that path, too.

Here's another example, less dramatic than divorce. Do you fly much? Maybe going to a conference or a business meeting? Perhaps you buy a drink or a meal or pay for headphones to watch a movie. Well, now the stranger sitting next to you is

30 percent more likely to make a similar purchase. If they're actually a friend or family member, the odds of them making a similar purchase doubles. That's the conclusion of a Stanford University researcher after looking at the in-flight purchase receipts of 250,000 passengers (Gardete 2015).

And even suicide is contagious. Public health experts have long studied a phenomenon known as "suicide clusters"—an unusually large number of suicides that take place in a short period of time, in a close geographic area. Suicide is the second-leading cause of death for Americans between ages fifteen to twenty-four, and the US Centers for Disease Control estimates that 1 percent to 5 percent of these suicides are the result of social contagion (Mohney 2016). Like the flu, suicidal ideation and acts can ripple out and spread to others nearby.

Feel like adding an extra ten minutes to your daily run? You've just influenced your runner friends to add three minutes to their normal run. A pair of researchers at MIT analyzed over one million runners over a five-year period of time (the runners were all logging their runs on an online database and social network) (Aral and Nicolaides 2017). They found that when someone ran an extra kilometer their friends increased their own runs by .3 kilometers. This ratio was the same for different metrics. If you run an extra ten minutes, I'll add three minutes to my own run. For every extra ten calories you burn, I'll end up burning three calories.

Are you a physician who decided to try out a new medical device, drug, or procedure? You've just influenced the other doctors in your area to do likewise. Researchers at Yale School of Medicine and Johns Hopkins School of Medicine conducted a five-year longitudinal study of surgeons who were treating women with breast cancer (Pollack et al. 2017). We can assume that doctors begin using a new device or test after considering medical evidence, insurance reimbursement, and patient requests. And using Medicare data, researchers found that when "early adopter" doctors began using somewhat controversial MRI and PET scans, peer physicians were twice as likely to begin using the test, too.

Friends, if leadership is influence, then leadership isn't a choice. You are always influencing those around you, whether you want to be or not. You are leading at work, and also at home. You lead your family and friends, and also strangers. The question is, are you influencing them—leading them—in a positive direction or a negative direction. Be mindful of your power as a leader. Lead with intent.

HOW MIGHT YOU APPLY THIS?

Just a few minutes ago, while still writing this chapter, I received an email from a listener of *The LEADx Leadership Show* who took my message to heart.

> I have been listening to your podcast for a couple of months now and love it. Listening to you reminded me of my roots in leadership and inspired me to work on inspiring one other person each day.
>
> I started, after being inspired by your podcast (and books) even though I am not a manager or team/group leader, to look sideways to the people around me and to try and find out how I can inspire them. Then the ceiling raised about 10 floors. I feel inspired by others and what they are going through and have tried to inspire them in return.
>
> Thank you, thank you, a thousand thank yous for inspir-

ing me to in turn inspire others. You are right that everyone
can be a leader by participating and engaging others.

Sincerely from the bottom of my heart, Matthew

You are a role model, whether you want to be or not. Your
emotions and actions cross over to those around you. Want
your teenagers to be safe drivers? Then you should never let
them see you text and drive. Want them to maintain a healthy
weight? Keep your own BMI in check. Wish your spouse was
more grateful for all that you do? Make sure you are expressing gratitude freely, too. Frustrated that your employees at work
show up late to meetings? Make sure you are always on time
(and close the door and start the presentation the very second
the meeting is supposed to begin). Want people to care about
the company? Ask about their kids and how they spent their
weekend so they know you care about them. Want your players
to show respect to the referees? Don't yell or curse at the refs
with every bad call.

And when you're feeling bored, a little down, unmotivated,
or even sad . . . that's the exact time you should look around at
others, and lead.

CONCLUSION

started this book with the assertion that leadership is a super-power. And we desperately need more superheroes.

A lack of workplace leadership contributes to 70 percent of employees not being engaged at work.

A lack of family leadership contributes to half the marriages in the US ending in divorce.

A lack of self-leadership contributes to obesity and substance abuse.

What we need is a real-world modern approach to management and leadership. Neither the command-and-control model of the industrial age nor the New Agey no-manager models of more recent times are effective.

Today's leaders need to focus on both people and profits; they should be measured on both retention and results. How do we reconcile this duality? We must throw out conventional management 101 lessons and embrace fresh, forward-looking tenets:

PRINCIPLE 1 Close Your Open Door Policy, fosters the autonomy and empowerment of team members and enables you to increase the amount of time you spend on deep work.

PRINCIPLE 2 Shut Off Your Smartphone, improves safety and focus among team members and leadership alike.

PRINCIPLE 3 Have No Rules, shifts your focus from enforcement to hiring, values, and guardrails—all of which in turn yield greater accountability and engagement.

PRINCIPLE 4 Be Likable Not Liked, ensures there is just enough separation for you to make tough decisions and to give candid feedback, without you having to be the jerk at work.

PRINCIPLE 5 Lead with Love, is a reminder that you don't need to like someone in order to care about them deeply—and caring drives engagement and loyalty.

PRINCIPLE 6 Crowd Your Calendar, reflects the reality that every minute wasted is a minute that can't be spent coaching team members or working on your most important tasks.

PRINCIPLE 7 Play Favorites, enables individuals to leverage their strengths and also gives you the flexibility to retain top performers.

PRINCIPLE 8 Reveal Everything (Even Salaries), enables team members to move fast, adapt to change, and make wise decisions and reduces their need to knock on your door with "got a minute" questions.

PRINCIPLE 9 Show Weakness, contributes to a culture of psychological safety and trust, thus reducing the magnitude of mistakes and fostering innovation.

PRINCIPLE 10 Leadership Is Not a Choice, reminds you that there are no time-outs in leadership; stay in your office or walk around, say good morning or keep your head down, maintain your values or ignore them—you are always leading.

FINALLY, GREAT LEADERS CARE. *You* care, otherwise you wouldn't be reading this book. And when you put this book down you do have a choice to make. Will you live your life on autopilot, or will you *lead with intent*? Remember, leadership = influence. You are influencing—leading—those around you whether you want to be or not. The question is: Are you leading in a positive direction or you are leading in a negative direction? The choice is yours.

How will you lead today?

RESOURCES

To download the *Great Leaders Have No Rules* Action Plan and Discussion Guide visit:

www.LEADx.org/actionplan

If you would like to stand out and get ahead in your career, LEADx offers free on-demand training in management fundamentals, leadership, productivity, communication, personal branding, and more. To check out the free daily training visit:

www.LEADx.org

ABOUT LEADX

What if every one of your managers had their own executive coach? Introducing Coach Amanda, the world's first executive coach powered by AI. Organizations use the LEADx platform to increase managerial competence, employee engagement, and productivity. Founded in 2017 and trusted by Fortune 500 companies, LEADx provides members with on-demand access to a suite of tools including adaptive assessments, directed learning paths, microlearning courses, and AI-powered executive coach bots. Don't all your managers deserve their own coach?

www.LEADx.org

ACKNOWLEDGMENTS

First, I'd like to thank Lolly Daskal for introducing me to my agent, Giles Anderson.

I'd like thank Giles for his tenacity and wisdom, which eventually led to this book deal.

Thank you to all my LEADx colleagues who are innovating leadership development solutions as we advance in our mission to spark one hundred million leaders around the world.

Thanks to my *LEADx Leadership* podcast guests for selflessly giving their time and advice: Morra Aarons-Mele, Heide Abelli, Jerry Acuff, Jon Acuff, Radha Agrawal, Aron Ain, Alan Alda, Delisa Alexander, Erika Andersen, Vernice Armour, Cam Awesome, Dick Axelrod, Paul Axtell, Patty Azzarello, John Baldoni, Craig Ballantyne, Justin Bariso, Luke Barnett, Dov Baron, Susan Baroncini-Moe, Thomas Barta, Alicia Bassuk, Mark Batterson, Dr. Stan Beecham, Vic Belonogoff, Beth

Beutler, Ken Blanchard, Rene Boer, Kris Boesh, Gary Brackett, Michael Breus, Judson Brewer, Patrick Brigger, Michael Bungay Stanier, David Burkus, Joe Byerly, Evan Carmichael, Carter Cast, Daniel Chard, Subir Chowdhury, Dorie Clark, Gary Cohen, Alisa Cohn, Rachel Cooke, David Covey, Jennifer Cue, Andy Cunningham, Lolly Daskal, Susan David, Dan Diamond, Robin Dreeke, Chris Ducker, Ann Dunwoody, Andre Durand, Dina Dwyer-Owens, David Dye, Chris Edmonds, Ellen Ensher, Bill Erickson, Leland Faust, Jody Foster, Susan Fowler, Erica Ariel Fox, Jason Fried, Jon Gordon, Jeff Haden, Morten T. Hansen, Sally Helgensen, Daisy Hernandez, Cameron Herold, Naphtali Hoff, Bryce Hoffman, Sally Hogshead, Ryan Holiday, Robb Holman, Dave Hopson, Karin Hurt, Khe Hy, Tiffany Jana, Leila Janah, Jathan Janove, Whitney Johnson, John Jonas, Michelle Joy, Shawn Kanungo, Karl Kapp, Amy Kates, Robbie Kellman-Baxter, Carrie Kerpen, Dave Kerpen, Matt Kincaid, Monica Klausner, Corey Kupfer, Lisa Lai, Mary Lamia, Abby Lawson, Andy Levitt, Elizabeth Lindsey, Scott Love, Mark Mader, Paul Marciano, Sara Margulis, David Marquet, Leigh Marz, Patty McCord, Mike McDerment, Daniel McGinn, Annie McKee, Doug McKenna, Bonnie Micheli, Donald Miller, G. Riley Mills, Christie Mims, Kathryn Minshew, Andy Molinsky, Angie Morgan, Amy Morin, Eric Mosley, Dave Munson, Tanveer Naseer, Dan Negroni, Tara-Nicholle Nelson, Rachael O'Meara, Barbara Oakley, Betty Palm, John Parker, Ben Parr, Andy Paul, Marilyn Paul, Rajeev Peshawaria, Joel Peterson, Dan Pink, Dan Pontefract, Christine Porath, Michael Port, Rhett Power, Skip Prichard, Jonathan Raymond, Nate Regier, Tom Reilly, James Robbins, Dan Rockwell, Tracy Roemer, John Rossman, Shelley Row, Chuck Runyon, Christina Russell, Jan Rutherford, MJ Ryan, Wendy Sachs, Jeff Sanders, Tim Sanders, Dave Sanderson, Greg Satell, Carl Schramm, Kim Scott, Patricia Scott, Steve Scott, Tina Seelig, Jason Selk, Jeremy Slate, Emily Smith, Hyrum Smith, Paul Smith, Andrew Sobel, Michael Sonnenfeldt, Sharon Spano, Joshua Spodek, Mike Steib, Gretchen Steidle, Sully Sullenberger, Jay Sullivan, Shelly Sun, Justin Talbot-Zorn, Connie Tang, Karissa Thacker, Maura Thomas, Mike Tippets, Bruce Tulgan, Dave Ulrich, Rory Vaden, Mike Vardy, Sarah Vermunt, Chris Voss, Cy Wakeman, Ron Warren, Peter Waszkiewicz, Michael Watkins, Jim Whitehurst, Scott Wintrip, Christopher Wirth, Liz Wiseman, Monica Worline, Gabriel Wyner, Denise Lee Yohn, Jill Young, and Kay Zanotti.

Finally, I'd like to thank the LEADx VIP community for all their support and getting the word out, especially in our early days: Adam Morris, Adam Olsen, Aideen Brennan, Alessandro Motroni, Alex Day, Ali Dahab, Alonso Castañeda, Andrew Mackay, Andy Storch, Andy Willingham, Василий Ларионов, Becky Beasley, Bethany Tahon, Bijay Limbu, Bill Barnes, Bob Casey, Brandon Trahan, Brett Angus, Brian Dunworth, Brian Lott, Calv Ng, Carl Hansen, Carlo D'Amico, Cathy Cagle, Cathy Tedesco, Chad Washam, Chidozie Moore Ekeanyanwu, Chito Mallillin, Chris Davis, Chris Edmonds, Chris Mayer, Chrissie Reynolds, Christopher Lewis, Chuck Roberson, Cole Dailey, Craig Douglas, Dan Milnor, Dan Wilson, Danielle Luigart, Darren Horne, Darren Tanner, Daryl Nauman, David Hackler, Deacon James, Dean Morbeck, Debra Wilson Hope, Diana Smeland, Diane Mobley, Don Maclaren, Don Polley, Ebong Eno, Eddy Piasentin, Ehsan Rasul, Emily Day, Eric David Jackson, Eric Puff, Erin Elizabeth, Frank Hoffman, Gail Nelson, Gisclerc Morisset, Glynnis Richardson, Greg Lauer, Gregg Taylor, Hassan Megahy, Heather Gale, Heather Speakman Morrison, James Lamb, James Nickle, James Skweres, Jamie Alford, Janine Blackburn, Jason Clayton, Jason Isaac, Jason Tremere, Jeff Davis, Jeff Miller, Jeff Moore, Jeff Rowell, Jennifer Carson, Jessica Hill, Jessica Paske-Driscoll, Jo Letty, Joe Groenhof, John Coakley Jr., John Moller, John Murphy, Jonathan Black, Joseph Rich, Julian E. Kaufmann, Kamal Jaroor, Kaoru Sato Miller, Karen Dimmick, Katie Kinnaman, Kelly Chau, Kenny Febers, Kevin Wan, Kim Weaver, Kris Painter, Kristine McFerren Daly, Kristof Maeyens, Laura Donnelly, Lauren Nicolette, Leland Vogel, Lemuel Goltiao, Leonard Brown, Lesley McCoy, Linda Kapembeza, Linda Lieratore, Lisa Brooks Ferguson, Lisa Day, Lisa Zawrotny, Lucy Yan, Lynn Gunn, Lynn Peter, Lynne Yura, Madeleine Murray, Marcelo Reda, Marcos Delgado, Marcus Gullett, Margaret Coley Crowley, Marie Johnson, Mario Gonsales Ishikawa, Mark D. Jones, Mark Gilbert, Mark Howell, Mark Richardson, Mark Teel, Markus Rabello, Martin McGlynn, Matt Milne, Matt Sloniker, Matthew Walker, Megan Thiessen, Michael Barrett, Michael Cook, Michael Raymer, Michalina Kunecka, Miles Park, Molly Ford Beck, Muzaddid Rashdee, Nathan Shields, Nic Lewis, Nicholas Moon, Nick Davies, Nick Hendren, Nina Lorene Hermann, Padraig Ruane, Pat Bates, Patrick Lin, Patrick Mumba, Paul Keen, Paul Simkins Jr., Reba Bailey, Rich Manwell, Rob Calder, Rob Diefenderfer, Rob Palacios, Robert Bell, Roi Ben-Yehuda, Rolf Biernath, Rosemary Hopkins, Ross Loofbourrow, Roy Chong Rong Yao, Ruby Cherie, Russ Bush, Russell Bush, Russell Green, Sabita Limbu, Sajit Sam Abraham, San Teekasub, Sarah Bright, Sarah Dye, Scott Yates, Sean Leong, Sharon Green, Stef Stroobants, Stephanie Kaufman, Stephen

Stormonth, Steve Hand, Steve Nagy, T.C. Thompson, Ted Martin, Terri Keener, Thomas Christensen, Thomas Forbord Eikevik Koch, Tim Goldstein, Tim Pangburn, Tobey Mathas, Tonya Dunbar McKinney, Tricia Odell, Will Leighton, Yaqub Adesola, Yoann Hamon, and Zachary Ashby.

WORKS CITED

Adams, Bailey. 2014. *The Busy Person's Guide to the Done List.* San Francisco: I Done This, Kindle edition.

American Psychological Association. 2017. *Stress in America: Coping with Change. Stress in America Survey.* Washington: American Psychological Association.

Aral, Sinan, and Christos Nicolaides. 2017. "Exercise contagion in a global social network." *Nature Communications* (April): 14753.

Ariely, Dan. November 8, 2014. */r/IAmA*. https://www.reddit.com/r/IAmA/comments/2lmp1k/im_dan_ariely_duke_professor_of_behavioral/ (accessed October 1, 2017).

Aronson, Elliot, Ben Willerman, and Joanne Floyd. 1966. "The Effect of a Pratfall on Increasing Interpersonal Attractiveness." *Psychonomic Science* 4, no. 6 (June): 227–228.

Atienzo, Erika, Dilys Walker, Lourdes Campero, Hector Lamadrid-Figueroa, and Juan Pablo Gutiérrez. 2009. "Parent-

Adolescent Communication About Sex in Morelos, Mexico: Does It Impact Sexual Behaviour?" *The European Journal of Contraception & Reproductive Health* 14, no. 2 (April): 111–119.

Atlassian. n.d. "You Waste a Lot of Time at Work." https://de.atlassian.com/time-wasting-at-work-infographic (accessed October 1, 2017).

Baron, Dov, interview by Kevin Kruse. March 29, 2017. "The #1 Secret to Engaging and Retaining Millennials from Dov Baron." *The LEADx Leadership Show.*

Barsade, Sigal G., and Olivia A. O'Neill. 2014. "What's Love Got to Do with It? A Longitudinal Study of the Culture of Companionate Love and Employee and Client Outcomes in a Long-Term Care Setting." *Administrative Science Quarterly* 59, no. 4 (May): 551–598.

Bethea, Charles. March 27, 2014. "The 25-Year-Old at the Helm of Lonely Planet." https://www.outsideonline.com/1922236/25-year-old-helm-lonely-planet (accessed October 1, 2017).

Bevins, Frankki, and Aaron. De Smet. January 2013. "Making Time Management the Organization's Priority." http://www.mckinsey.com/business-functions/organization/our-insights/making-time-management-the-organizations-priority (accessed October 1, 2017).

Boesch, Kris. 2017. *Culture Works: How to Create Happiness in the Workplace.* Denver: First Kalina Publishing.

Boesch, Kris, interview by Kevin Kruse. June 22, 2017. "The Secret to a Joyful Workplace." *The LEADx Leadership Show.*

Borpuzari, Pranibihanga. January 29, 2016. "Lifespan of Companies Shrinking to 18 Years: McKinsey's Dominic Barton." http://economictimes.indiatimes.com/small-biz/hr-leadership/lifespan-of-companies-shrinking-to-18-years-

mckinseys-dominic-barton/articleshow/50775384.cms
(accessed October 1, 2017).

Brackett, Gary, interview by Kevin Kruse. September 11, 2017.
"NFL Superstar Gary Brackett's Secret to Never Giving Up."
The LEADx Leadership Show.

Branson, Richard. April 6, 2015. "Why You Should Stand Up in
Meetings." https://www.virgin.com/richard-branson/why-you-
should-stand-meetings (accessed October 1, 2017).

Brooks, Brandon, interview by Kevin Kruse. April 2, 2017.

Campbell, Joseph. 1973. *The Hero with a Thousand Faces.*
Princeton: Princeton University Press.

CareerBuilder. June 9, 2016. "New CareerBuilder Survey
Reveals How Much Smartphones Are Sapping Productivity
at Work." http://www.careerbuilder.com/share/aboutus/
pressreleasesdetail.aspx?sd=6%2F9%2F2016&id=pr954&ed=
12%2F31%2F2016 (accessed October 1, 2017).

Chapman, Gary. 2015. *The 5 Love Languages; The Secret to Love
that Lasts.* Chicago: Northfield Publishing.

Chow, Andrew. December 23, 2011. "Distracted Doctors Linked
to Medical Errors." http://blogs.findlaw.com/injured/2011/12/
distracted-doctors-linked-to-medical-errors.html (accessed
October 1, 2017).

Christakis, Nicholas, and James Fowler. 2008. "The Collective
Dynamics of Smoking in a Large Social Network." *New
England Journal of Medicine* (May): 2249–2258.

Cooper, Anderson. April 9, 2017. "What is 'Brain Hacking'? Tech
Insiders on Why You Should Care." https://www.cbsnews
.com/news/brain-hacking-tech-insiders-60-minutes/ (accessed
October 1, 2017).

Coughlin, Tom. 2014. *Earn the Right to Win:How Success in
Any Field Starts with Superior Preparation.* New York City:
Portfolio.

Dale, Greg. n.d. "Duke Men's Basketball Coach Mike Krzyzewski on Coaching." http://www.championshipcoachesnetwork.com/public/249.cfm (accessed October 1, 2017).

Dalio, Ray. April 2017. "How to Build a Company Where the Best Ideas Win." https://www.ted.com/talks/ray_dalio_how_to_build_a_company_where_the_best_ideas_win (accessed October 1, 2017).

de Jager, Peter. December 3, 2003. "The Privacy Contradiction." December 3, 2003. https://www.theglobeandmail.com/technology/the-privacy-contradiction/article1169510 (accessed October 1, 2017).

Deloitte. 2015. *2015 Global Mobile Consumer Survey: US Edition.* New York City: Deloitte.

Detert, James R., and Amy C. Edmondson. May 2007. "Why Employees Are Afraid to Speak." https://hbr.org/2007/05/why-employees-are-afraid-to-speak (accessed October 1, 2017).

Doshi, Hiren, interview by Kevin Kruse. August 3, 2017.

Dwyer-Owens, Dina, interview by Kevin Kruse. August 8, 2017. "The Key to Amazing Work Culture Lies in Company Values." *The LEADx Leadership Show.*

Edelman. January 15, 2017. *2017 Edelman Trust Barometer.* https://www.edelman.com/trust2017/ (accessed October 1, 2017).

Eisenberg, Marla E., Dianne Neumark-Sztainer, Jayne A. Fulkerson, and Mary Story. 2008. "Family Meals and Substance Use: Is There a Long-Term Protective Association?" *Journal of Adolescent Health* 43: 151–156.

Eisenberg, Marla, Dianne Neumark-Sztainer, and Shira Feldman. 2009. "Does TV Viewing During Family Meals Make a Difference in Adolescent Substance Use?" *Preventive Medicine* 48, no. 6 (June): 585–587.

Ellison, Brenna. 2014. "Group Ordering Behavior in Food Choice Decisions." *Food Quality and Preferance* 37 (April): 79–86.

eMarketer. 2017. *Worldwide Ad Spending: The eMarketer Forecast for 2017.* New York: eMarketer.

Figliuolo, Mike. January 24, 2017. "How Comfortable Are You Being Vulnerable with Your Team Members?" https://www.smartbrief.com/original/2017/01/how-comfortable-are-you-being-vulnerable-your-team-members (accessed October 1, 2017).

Flacy, Mike. March 21, 2012. "Texting While Walking Claims Another Victim, Woman Falls Off Pier." https://www.digitaltrends.com/mobile/texting-while-walking-claims-another-victim-woman-falls-off-pier/ (accessed October 1, 2017).

———. September 27, 2012. "Woman Falls Off Cliff While Texting." https://www.digitaltrends.com/mobile/woman-falls-off-cliff-while-texting/ (accessed October 1, 2017).

Flood, Brian. January 3, 2017. "Rockettes Management Blasts 'Deceitful and Cowardly' Dancer for Secretly Recording Team Meeting." http://www.thewrap.com/rockettes-marie-claire-tolerate-intolerance-madison-square-garden-recording/ (accessed October 1, 2017).

Fox News. February 9, 2007. "Students Secretly Taping Angry Teachers." http://www.foxnews.com/story/2007/02/09/students-secretly-taping-angry-teachers.html (accessed October 1, 2017).

Frank, Reuben. December 14, 2016. "Anxiety Condition Caused Football-Obsessed Brandon Brooks to Miss Games." http://www.csnphilly.com/philadelphia-eagles/anxiety-condition-caused-football-obsessed-brandon-brooks-miss-games (accessed October 1, 2017).

Fulkerson, Jayne A., Mary Story, Alison Mellin, Nancy
Leffert, Dianne Neumark-Sztainer, and Simone A. French.
2006. "Family Dinner Meal Frequency and Adolescent
Development: Relationships with Developmental Assets and
High-Risk Behaviors." *Journal of Adolescent Health* 39:
337–345.

Gallup. February 11, 2010. "Saving Campbell Soup Company.
"*Gallup Management Journal.* http://news.gallup.com/
businessjournal/125687/saving-campbell-soup-company.aspx
(accessed October 1, 2017).

Gallup. 2017. *State of the American Workplace 2017.* Lincoln:
Gallup.

Gardete, Pedro M. 2015. "Social Effects in the In-Flight
Marketplace: Characterization and Managerial Implications."
Journal of Marketing Research 52, no. 3 (June): 360–374.

Gascoigne, Joel. June 22, 2016. "Tough News: We've Made 10
Layoffs. How We Got Here, the Financial Details and How
We're Moving Forward." https://open.buffer.com/layoffs-and-
moving-forward/ (accessed October 1, 2017).

Gascoigne, Joel, and Leo Widrich. November 24, 2015.
"Introducing the New Buffer Salary Formula, Calculate-Your-
Salary App and the Whole Team's New Salaries. "https://
open.buffer.com/transparent-salaries/ (accessed October 1,
2017).

Goldsmith, Marshall. April 23, 2010. "Empowering Your
Employees to Empower Themselves." https://hbr.
org/2010/04/empowering-your-employees-to-e (accessed May
2, 2017).

———. 2007. *What Got You Here Won't Get You There.* New York
City: Hachette Books.

Gregorian, Dareh. September 2, 2016. "Ex-Fox Anchor Gretchen
Carlson Secretly Recorded Meetings with Roger Ailes,

Caught 'Numerous Incidents' of Harassment on Tape." http://
www.nydailynews.com/news/national/gretchen-carlson-
secretly-recorded-meetings-roger-ailes-article-1.2776032
(accessed October 1, 2017).

Griswold, Alison. March 3, 2014. "Here's Why Whole Foods
Lets Employees Look Up Each Other's Salaries." http://
www.businessinsider.com/whole-foods-employees-have-open-
salaries-2014-3 (accessed October 1, 2017).

Hansson, David Heinemeier. July 27, 2017. "How We Pay People
at Basecamp." https://m.signalvnoise.com/how-we-pay-
people-at-basecamp-f1d04f4f194b (accessed October 1, 2017).

Harter, James, Frank Schmidt, Emily Killham, and James
Asplund. n.d. "Q12 Meta-Analysis." https://strengths.
gallup.com/private/resources/q12meta-analysis_flyer_
gen_08%2008_bp.pdf (accessed October 1, 2017).

Hass, Nancy. January 29, 2013. "And the Award for the next
HBO Goes to . . ." https://www.gq.com/story/netflix-founder-
reed-hastings-house-of-cards-arrested-development?mobify=0
(accessed October 1, 2010).

Hastings, Reed. August 1, 2009. "Netflix Culture: Freedom
& Responsibility." *SlideShare.* https://www.slideshare.net/
reed2001/culture-1798664 (accessed October 1, 2017).

Hermans, Roel, Anna Lichtwarck-Aschoff, Kirsten Bevelander,
Peter C. Herman, Junilla K. Larsen, and Rutger Engels.
2012. "Mimicry of Food Intake: The Dynamic Interplay
between Eating Companions." *PLoS ONE* 7, no. 2
(February).

Hermans, Roel, Junilla Larsen, Peter C. Herman, and Rutger
Engels. 2012. "How Much Should I Eat? Situational Norms
Affect Young Women's Food Intake During Meal Time."
British Journal of Nutrition 107, no. 4: 588–594.

Hetrick, Randy, interview by Kevin Kruse. September 27, 2016.

Hill, Karl, David Hawkins, Richard Catalano, Robert Abbott, and Jie Guo. 2005. "Family Influences on the Risk of Daily Smoking Initiation." *Journal of Adolescent Health* 37, no. 3: 202–210.

Hillan, Michael, interview by Kevin Kruse. August 3, 2017.

Inside Edition. June 25, 2015. "Doctor Caught Sexting During Stomach Surgery." http://www.insideedition.com/investigative/10895-doctor-caught-sexting-during-stomach-surgery (accessed October 1, 2017).

K. April 14, 2012. "Fleet Marine Life #144—Open Door." http://www.fleetmarinelife.com/?comic=fleet-marine-life-144-open-door (accessed May 2, 2017).

Karofsky, Peter S., Lan Zeng, and Michael R. Kosorok. 2001. "Relationship Between Adolescent–Parental Communication and Initiation of First Intercourse by Adolescents." *Journal of Adolescent Health* 28, no. 1 (January): 41–45.

Karsan, Rudy, and Kevin Kruse. 2011. *We: How to Increase Performance and Profits Through Full Engagement.* Hoboken: Wiley.

Key-Roberts, Melinda. 2014. "Strengths-Based Leadership Theory and Development of Subordinate Leaders." *Military Review* (March-April): 4–13.

Kincaid, Matt, interview by Kevin Kruse. June 13, 2017. "The Secret to Getting Your Team's Honest Opinion."

Kouzes, James, and Barry Posner. 2017. *The Leadership Challenge: How to Make Extraordinary Things Happen in Organizations.* San Francisco: Jossey-Bass.

Krulak, Charles. 1999. "The Strategic Corporal: Leadership in the Three Block War." *Marine Corps Gazette* 83, no. 1.

Kruse, Kevin. 2015. *15 Secrets Successful People Know About Time Management.* Philadelphia: The Kruse Group.

Krzyzewski, Mike. 2001. *Leading with the Heart: Coach K's*

Successful Strategies for Basketball, Business, and Life. New York City: Warner Business Books.

———. 2010. *The Gold Standard: Building a World-Class Team.* New York City: Business Plus.

Lange, Jeva. January 27, 2017. "Secret Recording of Republicans' Closed-Door Meeting Reveals Fears about Repealing ObamaCare." http://theweek.com/speedreads/676476/secret-recording-republicans-closeddoor-meeting-reveals-fears-about-repealing-obamacare (accessed October 1, 2017).

LCDR. 2016. "How Open Is the Open-Door Policy." https://www.rallypoint.com/answers/how-open-is-the-open-door-policy (accessed October 1, 2017).

Le Bon, Gustave. 2002. *The Crowd: A Study of the Popular Mind.* Mineola: Dover Publications.

Mark, Gloria, Daniela Gudith, and Ulrich Klocke. 2008. "The Cost of Interrupted Work: More Speed and Stress." *Conference on Human Factors in Computing Systems—Proceedings* (January): 107–110.

Maxwell, John. April 12, 2016. "The Key to Gaining Influence Is Earning It, Not Borrowing It." http://www.johnmaxwell.com/blog/the-key-to-gaining-influence-is-earning-it-not-borrowing-it (accessed October 1, 2017).

McChrystal, General Stanley. 2015. *Team of Teams: New Rules of Engagement for a Complex World.* New York City: Portfolio.

McChrystal, Stanley. March 2014. "The Military Case for Sharing Knowledge." https://www.ted.com/talks/stanley_mcchrystal_the_military_case_for_sharing_knowledge/transcript?language=en (accessed October 1, 2017).

McCord, Patty. January 2014. "How Netflix Reinvented HR." https://hbr.org/2014/01/how-netflix-reinvented-hr (accessed October 1, 2017).

McDermott, Rose, James H. Fowler, and Nicholas A. Christakis. 2013. "Breaking Up Is Hard to Do, Unless Everyone Else Is Doing It Too: Social Network Effects on Divorce in a Longitudinal Sample." *Social Forces* 92, no. 2 (December): 491–519.

Miller, K. A., M. L. Levin, D. J. Whitaker, and X. Xu. 1998. "Patterns of Condom Use Among Adolescents: The Impact of Mother-Adolescent Communication." *American Journal of Public Health* 88, no. 10 (October): 1542–1544.

Mirnig, Nicole, Gerald Stollnberger, Markus Miksch, Susanne Stadler, Manuel Giuliani, and Manfred Tscheligi. 2017. "To Err Is Robot: How Humans Assess and Act toward an Erroneous Social Robot." *Frontiers in Robotics and AI* (May): 21.

Mohney, Gillian. February 16, 2016. "Disturbing Suicide Cluster Prompts CDC to Start Investigation in Palo Alto." http://abcnews.go.com/Health/disturbing-suicide-cluster-prompts-cdc-start-investigation-palo/story?id=36953874 (accessed October 1, 2017).

Mueller, Pam A., and Daniel M. Oppenheimer. 2014. "The Pen Is Mightier Than the Keyboard: Advantages of Longhand Over Laptop Note Taking." *Psychological Science* 25, no. 6 (April): 1159–1168.

Munson, Dave, interview by Kevin Kruse. September 13, 2017. "Leadership at Saddleback Leather." *The LEADx Leadership Show.*

National Rifle Association. 2015. "Form 990." *Foundation Center.* http://990s.foundationcenter.org/990_pdf_archive/530/530116130/530116130_201512_990O.pdf (accessed October 1, 2017).

Newcomer, Eric. February 28, 2017. "In Video, Uber CEO Argues with Driver Over Falling Fares." https://www.bloomberg.com/news/articles/2017–02–28/in-video-uber-ceo-argues-with-driver-over-falling-fares (accessed October 1, 2017).

Oppezzo, Marily, and Daniel Schwartz. 2014. "Give Your Ideas Some Legs: The Positive Effect of Walking on Creative Thinking." *Journal of Experimental Psychology: Learning Memory, and Cognition* 40, no. 4: 1142–1152.

Oprah.com. January 15, 2010. "The Billion-Dollar Man." http://www.oprah.com/oprahshow/avatars-james-cameron/all (accessed October 1, 2017).

Peck, Emily. April 9, 2015. "Why Walking Meetings Can Be Better Than Sitting Meetings." http://www.huffingtonpost.com/2015/04/09/walking-meetings-at-linke_n_7035258.html (accessed October 1, 2017).

Pollack, Craig E., et al. 2017. "The Impact of Social Contagion on Physician Adoption of Advanced Imaging Tests in Breast Cancer." *Journal of the National Cancer Institute* 109, no. 8 (August).

Pope, Emily. October 8, 2015. "How General McChrystal Captures the Magic of Small Teams at Scale." https://generalassemb.ly/blog/how-general-stanley-mcchrystal-captures-the-magic-of-small-teams-at-scale (accessed October 1, 2017).

Preuss, Andreas. April 10, 2017. "Woman Falls Off California's Highest Bridge While Taking Selfie." http://www.cnn.com/2017/04/06/us/woman-falls-off-bridge-taking-selfie-trnd/index.html (accessed October 1, 2017).

Quinn, Rob. December 28, 2015. "Distracted Man Who Fell Off Cliff Identified." https://www.usatoday.com/story/news/nation/2015/12/28/san-diego-cliff-death-victim/77969662 (accessed October 1, 2017).

Rost, Joseph C. 1993. *Leadership for the Twenty-First Century.* Santa Barbara: Praeger.

Schawbel, Dan. April 21, 2013. "Bren Brown: How Vulnerability Can Make Our Lives Better." https://www.forbes.com/sites/danschawbel/2013/04/21/brene-brown-how-vulnerability-can-make-our-lives-better/#7e018e8536c7 (accessed October 1, 2017).

Semler, Ricardo. October 2014. "How to Run a Company with (Almost) No Rules." https://www.ted.com/talks/ricardo_semler_how_to_run_a_company_with_almost_no_rules (accessed October 1, 2017).

———. January 1994. "Why My Former Employees Still Work for Me." https://hbr.org/1994/01/why-my-former-employees-still-work-for-me (accessed October 1, 2017).

Sen, Bisakha. 2010. "The Relationship Between Frequency of Family Dinner and Adolescent Problem Behaviors After Adjusting for Other Family Characteristics." *Journal of Adolescence* 33, no. 1 (February): 187–196.

Shebloski, B., K. J. Conger, and K. F. Widaman. 2005. "Reciprocal Links Among Differential Parenting, Perceived Partiality, and Self-Worth: A Three-Wave Longitudinal Study." *Journal of Family Psychology* 19, no. 4: 633–642.

Shephard, Dave. June 17, 2014. "Re: Commander's Open Door Policy." https://www.rallypoint.com/answers/commander-s-open-door-policy (accessed May 2, 2017).

Sierra Club. 2015. "Form 990." *Sierra Club.* https://www.sierraclub.org/sites/www.sierraclub.org/files/Sierra%20Club%202015_IRS%20F990_FINAL_PUBLIC%20DISCLOSURE%20COPY.pdf (accessed October 1, 2017).

Simonton, Ben, interview by Kevin Kruse. August 3, 2017.

Smith, Sam. 1993. *The Jordan Rules.* Chicago: Pocket Books.

Sondheimer, Eric. April 27, 2017. "Listen Up, Coaches: Watch Out for Hidden Recording Devices." http://www.latimes.com/sports/highschool/varsity-times/la-sp-coach-recordings-sondheimer-20170427-story.html (accessed October 1, 2017).

Stack, Jack. 2013. *The Great Game of Business.* New York City: Crown Business.

Stothart, C., A. Mitchum, and C. Yehnert. 2015. "The Attentional Cost of Receiving a Cell Phone Notification." *Journal of Experimental Psychology: Human Perception and Performance* 41, no. 4: 893–897.

Sullenberger, Chesley, interview by Kevin Kruse. July 28, 2017. "Leadership Lessons from the Miracle on the Hudson." *The LEADx Leadership Show.*

Suster, Mark. May 13, 2010. "Entrepreneurs Should Be Respected, Not Loved." https://bothsidesofthetable.com/entrepreneurs-should-be-respected-not-loved-94677205d1c9#.oxglufme3 (accessed October 1, 2017).

Talev, Margaret, and Carol Hymowitz. April 30, 2014. "Executives Say Walking During Meetings Leads to Good Decision-Making." http://mashable.com/2014/04/30/walking-meetings-decision-making/#5kZjtFmPCaqE (accessed October 1, 2017).

The Office: "Fun Run." 2007. Directed by Greg Daniels. Performed by Steve Carell.

Tornielli, Andrea. July 14, 2017."The 'No Complaining' Sign at Pope Francis' Door." http://www.lastampa.it/2017/07/14/vaticaninsider/eng/the-vatican/the-no-complaining-sign-at-pope-francis-door-VNoj5P7UruA5RN5a1VlLjL/pagina.html (accessed October 1, 2017).

Tracy, Marc. October 15, 2016. "Houston's Coach Pecks Away at Football's Macho Culture, a Kiss at a Time." *New York Times.*

US Army. 2014. *Army Command Policy: Army Regulation 600–20.* Washington, DC: US Army.

Vaden, Rory, interview by Kevin Kruse. March 9, 2017. "Rory Vaden's 5 Steps to Multiply Your Time." *The LEADx Leadership Show.*

Van Natta Jr, Don. April 3, 2013. "Video Shows Mike Rice's Ire." https://youtube/52YIen9A_dc (accessed May 2, 2017).

Wagmeister, Elizabeth. May 11, 2017. "Steve Harvey's Shocking Memo to Talk Show Staff Surfaces." http://variety.com/2017/tv/news/steve-harvey-memo-staff-talk-show-1202423077/ (accessed October 1, 2017).

Wakeman, Cy, interview by Kevin Kruse. July 12, 2017. "How to Eliminate Workplace Drama Once and for All." *The LEADx Show.*

———. 2010. *Reality-Based Leadership.* San Francisco: Jossey-Bass.

Ward, Adrian, Kristen Duke, Ayelet Gneezy, and Maarten Bos. 2017. "Brain Drain: The Mere Presence of One's Own Smartphone Reduces Available Cognitive Capacity." *Journal of the Association for Consumer Research* 2, no. 2: 140–154.

Washington, Melvin C., Ephraim A. Okoro, and Peter W. Cardon. 2013. "Perceptions of Civility for Mobile Phone Use in Formal and Informal Meetings." *Business and Professional Communication Quarterly* (October): 52–64.

Weiner, Jeff. April 3, 2013. "The Importance of Scheduling Nothing." https://www.linkedin.com/pulse/20130403215758–22330283-the-importance-of-scheduling-nothing/ (accessed October 1, 2017).

Welch, Jack, and Suzy Welch. 2006. *Winning: The Answers.* New York City: HarperBusiness.

Wikipedia. n.d. *Criticism of Mother Teresa.* https://en.wikipedia.org/wiki/Criticism_of_Mother_Teresa (accessed October 1, 2017).

———. n.d. *Namaste.* https://en.wikipedia.org/wiki/Namaste (accessed October 1, 2017).

Wong, Leonard, and Stephen Gerras. 2015. *Lying to Ourselves: Dishonesty in the Army Profession.* Carlisle: US Army War College.

Wooden, John. 2005. *Wooden on Leadership: How to Create A Winning Organization.* New York: McGraw-Hill Education.

Zak, Paul. January-February 2017. "The Neuroscience of Trust." https://hbr.org/2017/01/the-neuroscience-of-trust (accessed October 1, 2017).

INDEX

ABOUT THE AUTHOR

Kevin Kruse is the founder and CEO of LEADx (leadx.org), the world's first conversational learning platform for leadership development, and the LEADx Academy, a free online education platform and company that provides leadership training to people in 192 countries. He is the host of the *LEADx Leadership* podcast, which has exceeded over a million downloads. Kevin is also a *New York Times* bestselling author of six books including *15 Secrets Successful People Know About Time Management* and *Employee Engagement 2.0*. His work has been featured in *Forbes, Fast Company,* the *New York Times,* and on Fox News. Kevin's views on leadership, productivity, and entrepreneurship have earned him invitations to speak to Fortune 500 executives, US Marine Corp officers, nonprofit leaders, and even members of Congress. His personal mission is, over the next ten years, to spark 100 million intentional leaders. When he's not writing, speaking, or leading, Kevin juggles life in Philadelphia as Dad to Amanda, Natalie, and Owen. Kevin Kruse invites readers to contact him at:

E-mail: kevin@leadx.org
Online: www.kevinkruse.com
LinkedIn: www.linkedin.com/in/kevinkruse67/
Facebook: www.facebook.com/KruseAuthor
YouTube: www.youtube.com/user/KruseAuthor
Instagram: https://www.instagram.com/kevinauthor/
Twitter: @Kruse